D0942361

Praise for *The Unbreakable Child*

"... a beautifully told story about strength and an enduring faith that can lead but one place: to forgiveness."
~ **Booklist (starred review)**

"*The Unbreakable Child* is an act of courage, a book that insists on the primacy of justice, no matter how long the delay. Kim Michele Richardson is one indestructible woman, and determined to give traumatic memories a rightful meaning,."
~ **Jason Berry**, author, *Vows of Silence*

"This is a gripping account not just of horrific betrayal but also of heroic recovery."
~ **David Clohessy**, director of SNAP and winner, *People Magazine*'s 25 Most Intriguing People in 2003

"Not so much a tragic tale as it is a testament to the resilience of human nature and the fighting spirit residing somewhere in each of us."
~ **Greg Barrett**, veteran journalist and author, *The Gospel of Father Joe*

"The most powerful story I've read in a long time. You'll feel her pain and her triumph, and be reminded that the human spirit is resilient beyond all reason. This book will change you."
~ **Jenna Glatzer**, author, *Celine Dion: For Keeps*

"A harrowing, but beautifully crafted saga of one woman's courageous fight against evil, and her victory over the greatest titan in history — the Catholic church. This is a book that will haunt you."
~ **Alanna Nash**, author, *The Colonel*

"Grim yet ultimately inspiring, this harrowing biography catalogues years of institutional abuse that took place in the Saint Thomas-Saint Vincent Orphan Asylum, a Catholic orphanage in Anchorage, Kentucky."
~ *Kentucky Examiner*

"A must read for students entering the field of social work! Thank you, Ms. Richardson, for opening your life and sharing your journey for our betterment."
~ **Dr. Eugene H. Foster**, former KY state child welfare executive.

"...one of the best and most disturbing books I have read in my life. Pain, despair, courage and hope fill every page...leaving the reader to better understand how abuse by religious leaders is easily swept under the rug and why it is one of the worst crimes imaginable. It should be required reading for parents, social workers and especially religious employees and volunteers of every denomination."
~ **Morris Dees**, Founder of The Southern Poverty Law Center and author, *A Lawyer's Journey, The Morris Dees Story, Hate on Trial, The Case Against America's Most Dangerous Neo-Nazi.*

"... a book that comes with a message from a Kentucky author and that has touched me more than any book I've read in the past year. Grim but ultimately inspiring."
~*THE NEWS-ENTERPRISE*, Elizabethtown KY, Mary Daugherty

"... one of the hardest books I've ever read, yet one of the most necessary. I am a Catholic nun and was outraged at the humiliation, degradation, pain and exploitation that Kim and the others experienced during their years at the orphanage. I am so very, very sorry that those who should have shown God's love for them treated them with such cruel intent. Kim's amazing journey of healing is ultimately a beacon of hope, showing that in our darkest moments our light shines brightest."
~ **Sr. Ann Marie Borgess**, Toledo Ohio

"Kim Michele Richardson's memoir tells two compelling stories. The first story covers her traumatic childhood of abuse at the hands of the nuns in charge of a Catholic orphanage in rural Kentucky. The second traces her quest for justice, on behalf of herself, her sister, and 40+ other orphans, through a lawsuit filed by William McMurry. Either story, standing alone, would command the reader's attention. Woven together, these stories reveal a quest for justice defined not so much by vindication or by monetary compensation, but rather by love." –
~ **James M. Chen**, Dean, University of Louisville Brandeis School of Law

For my Language Arts Class I had to read a book and make a poster. I picked The Unbreakable Child because it seemed like a good book and after reading it.... I decided it has to be one of the best. It showed me that life could be so much harder and I have great blessings in my life. And after reading it I just wanted to thank my mom.
~**A.T.**, age 16, Kenai, Alaska

"It's a gut-wrenching book but ... It delivers what the title promises..."
~**Writer's Digest**

". . . power of forgiveness is overwhelming in this book . . . a powerful, powerful story."
~ **WFIN Radio, Ohio**

The Unbreakable Child

by

Kim Michele Richardson

The Unbreakable Child
A story about forgiving the unforgivable
Kim Michele Richardson

Copyright © 2012 by Kim Michele Richardson
Cover design by Carolyn Sheltraw, csheltraw.com.
Author photo used with permission by Andrew Eccles,
Andrew Eccles, NY, NY.

All rights reserved. No part of this book may be reproduced or transmitted in any form or by any means, electronic or mechanical, including photocopying, recording, or by any informa- tion storage and retrieval system, without the written permission of the publisher, except where permitted by law.

Library of Congress Control Number: 2012919311

Richardson, Kim Michele.
The unbreakable child / by Kim Michele Richardson. -- 3rd ed.
ISBN-13: 978-0-615-71469-1 (pbk.)
ISBN-10: 0-615714-69-2 (pbk.)

Disclaimer: This is a work of non-fiction. All events, characters and situations described in it are real. In some instances the author may have taken liberties with chronology in the interest of narrative flow or changed names of persons in order to protect confidentiality, dignity, and respect.

THIRD EDITION

ISBN 13: 978-0-615-71469-1

Printed in the United States of America

www.theunbreakablechild.com

To my forever sisters

*And to the forty-four courageous plaintiffs,
former residents of Saint Thomas - Saint Vincent Orphanage,
and valiant lawyer William F. McMurry,
who, together, bravely stepped forward in 2004 to expose
and bring past injustices to light.*

Foreword by David Clohessy

Thanks for picking up this book. Now take the next crucial step and read it.

This is crucial because all of us should better understand the largely silent but devastating epidemic of child abuse.

Studies show that one in three girls and one in six boys will be abused. Imagine the depression, addictions, emotional trauma and physical ailments this causes for literally millions of kids, who are forced to carry these debilitating effects well into adulthood.

But there's another reason to read on. It's because victims of horrific childhood trauma can and do recover. Kim certainly has. And her struggle and triumph are both instructive and inspiring.

All of us can benefit from both parts of this gripping story: how innocent, trusting, vulnerable kids are abused, and how deeply wounded adults overcome unimaginable horror.

Most of us, of course, have never faced the abuse that Kim, her sisters, and likely dozens of other orphans faced at this allegedly caring "house of horrors." All of us, however, have faced, or will face adversity. We can learn how to keep our troubles in perspective and how to overcome them by reading of the courage, wisdom, and persistence of this extraordinarily brave and strong woman.

The experiences of Kim and her sisters, and the on-going revelations of crimes and cover-ups by clergy, serve to remind us that all individuals and institutions are flawed. Those most flawed are usually those imbued with considerable power that is sometimes ruthlessly exercised behind closed doors, while publicly honored and praised.

Whether we were raised in religious families or not, almost all of us have been taught to respect, even revere, spiritual authority figures. The inexcusable suffering of Kim and other orphans at this "home" serves as a painful reminder that even "good" people can do awful things, and that titles and positions can be mere facades for evil.

Fortunately, as a grown-up Kim had legal options that are, in the vast majority of cases, denied to child abuse victims. Despite Kentucky's predator-friendly laws (notably the archaic and arbitrary technicality called the statute of limitations), Kim and others were able to expose their predators by filing civil lawsuits.

For the few survivors who have this chance, taking legal action is usually very healing, especially in the long term. (In the short term, it can often be a draining and stressful emotional roller coaster ride.) Using the justice system to educate the public about child predators and their immoral enablers has another crucial benefit: it protects kids from future harm and deters otherwise reckless or callous employers and supervisors.

This foreword is very tough for me to write. I can't begin to match the adult Kim's eloquence. I can't imagine the young Kim's suffering. I can't fathom, even after reading this book, how Kim endured and ultimately overcame this horror.

I can, however, thank you for picking up this book, enthusiastically recommend it, pray that you'll read it and share it with others, and hope that you will take its vital lessons to heart, so that other kids will be spared the trauma visited upon these orphans.

~~~~~~~~~~~~~~~~~~

David Clohessy is the National Director of Survivors' Network of those Abused by Priests (SNAP), and was named *People* magazine's 25 "Most Intriguing People" in 2003.

Foreword by
Father Thomas Doyle, J.C.D., C.A.D.C.

"Bad girls go to hell!" The Unbreakable Child, p. 12. So said Sister Charlie to three-year-old Kim, a "resident" at St. Thomas/St Vincent Orphan Asylum, situated in rural Anchorage, Kentucky. Kim didn't have to become a bad girl, nor did she have to wait. She was already in hell.

The dissonance between the promises and preaching of the official Catholic Church and the horrors perpetrated against innocent children by some of its official representatives is far more than the average decent person can even imagine much less comprehend. Probably the worst experiences of these vicious and mind-bending horrors took place in orphanages founded and run by Catholic religious orders.

The Unbreakable Child is the story of an innocent child who not only survived her lengthy sojourn in this earth-bound hell, but emerged from it unbroken, destined to go on and accomplish the near-impossible. She and forty-four other survivors of the hell created by the Sisters of Charity of Nazareth found the courage and tenacity to stand up to the mighty institution of the Roman Catholic Church, demanding that the secret world of torture be exposed. They demanded justice and in so doing they unknowingly entered the final chapter of their abuse.

One would think that any organization, especially a Christian Church, would recoil in shock to learn that one of its own institutions, dedicated to the care of innocent children, was, in fact, submitting them to systematized abuse of unimaginable dimensions. Not so the official Catholic Church, in reality a monarchy the "leaders" of which have put the victims of their own abusive violence through additional re-victimization when faced with their demands for justice.

Kim and her fellow survivors of the Church's hell in rural Kentucky learned this. Her riveting tale of torture and abuse does not end with her liberation from the orphan asylum/gulag. She painfully takes the reader through her reactions to the impersonal and clearly unsympathetic legal process.

The Unbreakable Child also introduces the attorney who guided Kim and the others through the courts as they painstakingly sought justice. William McMurry may have initially viewed this case as another legal challenge, albeit a daunting one, but he soon became more than a lawyer. He became what the official Church never provided its own victims . . . a compassionate friend, a staunch advocate and above all, a champion for justice.

The Unbreakable Child is a true story that defies the comfortable yet unreal assumptions that the Catholic Church always means what it preaches and truly is a haven for those who are suffering, afraid, and alone. Kim's story goes beyond what one can imagine about life behind the door of the refuge for the innocent children left there. It is also a story of hope.

Not only did Kim Michele Richardson (and forty-four others) win a legal case, but she and they proved that the limits of human courage cannot be fathomed nor can the power of such courage ever be second-guessed. Kim took on the vast and mighty kingdom of the Catholic Church and won, in spite of its power, wealth, and influence.

The dark side of the Catholic Church, sexual and physical abuse by priests, was first exposed to the public twenty five years ago. *The Unbreakable Child* adds an even more mind and soul numbing dimension to this revelation; that of the physical, sexual, emotional, and spiritual abuse perpetrated on countless innocent children hidden behind the walls of the very institutions that promised them a home.

This book should be required reading for the church's bishops and religious superiors who continue to distance themselves from the harsh reality of the harm inflicted and covered up by their organization. It should also be read by the countless lay people who simply refuse to believe that such nightmares are made real.

The Unbreakable Child is the graphically true story of a girl who thought she was abandoned by God but in reality was saved by her own strength and courage.

~~~~~~~~~~~~~~~~~~~~~~

Father Thomas Doyle is a Canon lawyer who was previously on the payroll of the Vatican Embassy in Washington DC. Awarded the Cavallo Award for Moral Courage in 1992, the Priest of Integrity Award from Voice of the Faithful in 2002, and the Isaac Hecker Award from the Paulist Fathers in 2003. Doyle, a priest in the Dominican Order for the past 40 years, received an official commendation from the Order for his "prophetic work in drawing attention to clergy abuse and for advocating the rights of victims and abusers.

SAINT THOMAS - SAINT VINCENT
ORPHAN ASYLUM
ANCHORAGE KENTUCKY

Or-phan \ `or-fn\ n:
one deprived of some protection
or advantage

One

"I am not afraid of tomorrow,
for I have seen yesterday
and love today"

~William Allen White

Sister Charlie died the week I turned seven. Hate killed her, or so I'd heard. Whether it was hers or my own, I wasn't quite sure.

I remembered once, when I was just three years old, Sister Charlie found traces of soil in my panties. She dragged me to the toilet, ripped off my panties, and threw them in. She pushed me toward the bowl. It felt like she would snap my neck—my little hands couldn't fight her off. I opened my mouth to take a huge breath and she dunked my head and held it under, then brought me up for a gasp of air. I gagged at the stench and the feces I'd swallowed, and vomited. She dunked my head again.

With my face dripping, she dragged me back to the orphanage dayroom and thrashed my bare bottom with the thick, red paddleboard in front of everyone.

~~~

I knelt on the wooden prie-dieu and stared at the plain, pine coffin resting on the chapel altar. The hazy smoke of powerful incense curled to the ceiling. Through the incense I smelled the long-ago feces, vomit and rotting fruit. My feces and vomit. Her rotting-fruit body odor.

The altar was too high for me to see inside, even on tiptoe. I wondered if there was so much incense because she still stank like she did when she was alive. I wondered if God would thank her for being so strict with us orphans so we wouldn't go to Hell for being bad.

I wondered if the Devil had a special toilet prepared for her, with big strong assistant-devils who would dunk her head in feces and vomit every minute of eternity.

For three days the nuns herded us into the chapel to visit her body. And for two hours on each of those days, I knelt before dead Sister Charlie and worried about Hell. Hers and mine.

~~~

What was I doing here? My heart pounded as I reached for the knob. It had taken more than four decades to reach this door — this man. I stopped with one foot inside and one outside the plush attorney's office. I studied the chalked colors decorating the room. The walls seemed to bleed pastels. If this pricey attorney didn't have the taste to hire a decent decorator, how could I trust him with my case? With my life story? He wasn't the man for the job. Of course, I didn't think anyone was the person for the job. Some things were best left buried.

Before I could retreat, the secretary called out from her desk at the far end of the room. "Can I help you, Ma'am?"

I gritted my teeth, dragged myself the rest of the way into the room, and took a few short steps across the expanse of pale carpet. The secretary smiled. Her teeth were too white, just as the walls were too crayoned — too everything.

"My name is Kim. I have an appointment with Mr. McMurry."

"Yes, Ma'am, I'll let him know you're here. If you'd like to have a seat," she gestured toward the waiting area, "he'll be right with you."

I took the chair closest to the door. Reaching to the small table beside me, I picked up a magazine devoted to parachuting then put it down. A skydiving photo hung on the far wall. Hmm, a skydiving attorney? And I immediately pegged this man as arrogant and handsome with a type-A personality.

The inner door opened. William F. McMurry, attorney-at-law, strode toward me and extended his hand. Late-forties with a slow-dance toward fifty, though time had been gracious. His clothing screamed wealth, while his manner spoke class. The *good* kind of class money couldn't buy.

"Hello, Kim?"

In my mind, I stepped forward, driven by the need to expose injustices too long kept secret. In my heart I stepped back, desperate to protect my family and my hard-won happiness. Instead, I rose and met his hand with mine. "Mr. McMurry."

"Call me William." A youthful, warm smile reached his eyes.

No, I thought. I'll keep you at bay, keep the honorific for now.

"Mr. McMurry," I repeated, hinting at challenge by slightly raising a brow.

"Come on back, Kim. We'll use the conference room."

And stepping into that room with him meant stepping into a controversial lawsuit involving the abuse of forty-five former orphans by nuns and a priest of the Roman Catholic Church. Worse, it meant confronting my memories, which I'd shoeboxed and placed on my highest mental shelf.

I followed him into his room and took the seat he offered me. I placed two childhood photographs and a bracelet on the table. He closed the door and my heart slammed violently. What the hell was I doing here?

~~~

Long ago, the State of Kentucky declared my mother unfit and took custody of my three older sisters and me. Then it abandoned us to the brutal care of a Catholic orphanage, branding us eternally *orphan*.

Orphan. Was there a more lonesome word in the lexicon? Why had I promised to support my sister Caity? Let her drag me into this lawsuit? I wanted to help her, but at whose expense? I could change this path in a snap. Kiss fate and walk the less perilous path. One hiccup from McMurry and I'd bail. Just one. I searched his steel-gray eyes, waiting for the hiccup, but none came.

"Why don't you start at the beginning, Kim?"

How does one describe *evil*, and how does one explain the evils of those who wore the face of God, who cloaked evil with His veil?

I had always viewed my childhood as a separate being from my adulthood, taken a toddler's creed to never share, then finally tossed it like yesterday's garbage. It was 2004. I was a competent adult with a family of my own, years removed from my victimhood as the nuns' punching bag and the priest's target. The past had no power over me.

"Saint Thomas-Saint Vincent Orphan Asylum was founded decades before I arrived in 1960. The boys' wing was named Saint Thomas, the girls' side was known as Saint Vincent."

Mr. McMurry leaned in.

"It was located in Anchorage, Kentucky. The back hills, far away from polite society and prying eyes."

He reached for a file, pulled out a large picture and placed it in front of me.

"Saint Thomas." My gaze fixed on the three-story, brown brick building and I shivered. "I can still smell it. The institutional stink, bleach and disinfectants . . ." I crossed my arms to block the odor that seemed to suddenly seep into my skin, then ooze out and halo me with an infinite reek, as I thought it did when I'd lived there. I chewed on the corner of my lip and forced myself to study the picture of my Home-Sweet-Hell-Hole.

"They force-fed us." My voice cracked. "And the priest … the governing priest who ran the orphanage … He—" Words clogged.

"Father Lammers?"

"Yes. He had a mole on his hand." I tapped the top of mine. "He liked to touch with his hands, not his heart."

"Was there penetration?" he asked in a calm voice.

I took a deep calming breath, then another. It didn't help. My heart lunged and a sickening lump formed in my throat. I scrutinized the attorney. His eyes showed concern, but he didn't push. I didn't want this man, this attorney, to see my vulnerability or hear the fear in my voice. I was strong. I knew I was. Still, I turned away, ran my fingers through my hair, reached up to wipe unshed tears. And to no surprise, I found none. Someone had stolen my tears, and I needn't search too far to find the thieves.

There was no one left to punish. Sister Charlie, Father Lammers, all were dead. The abuses we'd suffered happened decades ago. I didn't want to punish and I didn't need or want the memories, monies, or conflicts that would come from trying.

Be strong, I told myself. Do it for Caity, Pamela and Gayla. And all the others.

My fears slowly dripped, pooling in puddles around me. I raised my fingers, wiped beads of sweat from my brow, then looked at the two photographs and the bracelet I'd plunked down on the conference table. It had been decades since I'd pulled them out. These three objects were the only tangible remains of my youth. The realization punched me in the gut. One of the photos depicted me standing in front of a large, weatherworn statue of the Blessed Virgin Mary. Another showed my First Holy Communion day. And Mrs. Lindauer, a State social worker, gave me the prized scarab bracelet when I turned eight years old.

I picked up the bracelet and rubbed a colored bead. My hand trembled. I curled my fingers around it to stop the shake.

Over thirty years ago I'd walked out of Saint Thomas Orphan Asylum-Saint Vincent Orphanage, and on that day, I took with me only the clothes on my back and my treasured scarab bracelet, hidden in my sock.

"This is all I have from my childhood," I said softly.

Saying so made it real. Next to memories, they were all I had to confirm that I even lived a childhood, and I couldn't destroy or give away the memories, even if I tried. Not that I hadn't.

"I contacted the archdiocese of Louisville, Kentucky and they said my early childhood photos and official documents had been destroyed, every one of them. I don't know whether they were destroyed to cover up abuses or merely as housecleaning. The nuns, they were brutal, vicious. Times were different. Sister Charlie was the worst." I shook my head slowly. "The priest, Father Lammers ..." The words felt heavy, my lips quivered. "It was painful. I was only seven."

I looked away, bit hard on my lip. To demand justice meant reliving the horrors. The beatings. The starvation. The force-fed drugs meant to keep us compliant.

I needed to do this. Be strong.

But still, I was afraid to speak, because speaking brings back voice. He waited, exhibited quiet compassion, interrupting only when necessary.

A forgotten childhood meant a lifetime of evasiveness with acquaintances: friends new and old, avoiding eye contact, and dancing around the subject of youth that others so freely shared.

I'd been running a long time not knowing where I was going, but I knew I had to come home. Someone had to bring me back, and destiny chose William McMurry. By the time I finished recounting and revealing, I was drenched in sweat, sitting on a pile of memories.

He leaned in. "Now there are a few papers you'll need to sign." He opened a manila folder at his elbow. "These will allow me to work on your behalf."

I took the pen he handed me and signed, but my head was far away from that modern, light-filled office. A nun's shrill voice was calling me a bad girl, telling me all bad girls go to Hell. A priest's soft hand unzipped his pants and—

The pen clattered to the table.

"Thank you for seeing me today, Mr. McMurry." I pushed back the chair. My stomach rolled, squeezed. I had to get out of here. "I'm afraid I have another appointment."

He nodded. "Do you have any questions, Kim?"

I gripped the chair's armrest. I'd come prepared with a test, to see if he was on the side of justice and not merely out for notoriety and the reward he could get from being the champion of innocents.

A simple question: Who wears the face of God?

But in the end I didn't ask. I hoped he knew the right answer. Right now my answers were queasy, threatening to spill. Be strong—mentally stronger than your body's physical response. Fight it. I took a slow, deep breath, released the tension in my fingers, sat up, and straightened my jacket.

I'm strong, I know I am, a functioning adult, not a five-year-old orphan. *Strong.* The nausea slowly faded, then stilled. I knew the abandonment of true Christian values, the subjection of helpless children to unspeakable horrors, were at long last being brought to justice, to the public's watchful eyes. And recently, a National spotlight had shone on William McMurry. He'd represented two hundred forty-two sexual abuse victims of the Catholic Church's ordained, successfully leading them to a magnanimous victory.

That we were orphans made this lawsuit different. Other victims of the Church had family to support and protect them. We had only ourselves, and the shared horror of our violated childhood.

Now Pandora's Box pulsed, threatened to explode secrets, as more and more victims came forward, hoping for their own miracles.

Still, I was scared. I didn't want to give this man my diary, to leave him with my most private words and secrets, to use however he chose to.

I suddenly felt soulless. And for one brief moment I reached back, to take back.

But it was too late.

Two
When is afternoon?

"Secret, secret," the little girl whispered in my ear. "Movie, but only if you're good." She poked her pudgy finger in my face.

I was trying especially hard to be good because it was movie day. I didn't want to miss Peter Pan's Never-Never Land. I moved away from the girl and toddled around St. Thomas's gunmetal-colored, concrete dayroom with a dozen other orphans. Pages of tattered books and a few old chewed-up wooden ABC blocks were strewn on the floor. I picked up a crumpled page. "I am three years old. One. Two. Three. Three Blind Mice. I'm not blind. I'm quiet. I'm a good girl. And good girls get to see *Peter Pan*." I stuffed the page back into a ratty book then set it on the floor.

My faded checkered dress hung loose on my tiny frame; its Peter Pan collar was stained and fell to one side, revealing my shoulder. I moved my bare feet in unnatural silence, stopped and ran my hands over my arms and legs. I shivered, looked down at a girl and shoved my arm in her face. "Peopley-bumps, see?"

My hair hung straggly just below my ears, and my bangs were razor cut with no definition. A comb or brush hadn't been taken to my blonde hair in days, and it stuck out untamed all over my head. My fingers were bloodied from the weekly nail clipping. The nuns habitually clipped our nails down to the quick: no stray edges to worry about. I sucked my finger and grimaced at its coppery flavor.

I stopped in front of a whispering toddler, pressed a finger against my lips, and blew a loud shush. The girl screwed up her face and reached for my hair. I elbowed her, narrowed my eyes in challenge, then backed away. I needed quiet. The others were noisy.

"I'm a good girl."

And when I'm a good girl I get fewer beatings.

The beatings were scary, but I was getting used to them. Waiting for them was scarier. The Sister of Charity in charge of my dormitory was Sister Charlie, a large nun with a large, round face covered with an angry permanence of red splotches. She had tight lips and slits for eyes. Hard, angry eyes.

Sister Charlie was very old and she stank. When she exhaled, her breath smelled like an old groundhog dying in a dairy barn. The smell frightened me. And worse, it lingered behind when she walked away.

I'd never seen her smile. Sometimes Sister Michael Anthony would come to the toddlers' dorm to help out, but she didn't smile either.

Yes, it would be much scarier if I missed the movie and had to stay alone with Sister Charlie.

Movies were a rare treat. A noisy, outdated projector would be set up to show the movie in Sabrina Hall, located in the damp bowels of Saint Thomas. There we would seat ourselves on cold concrete floors to be swept away to unimaginable lands, leaving behind the cruelty of our caregivers' whims.

I pulled myself up by the window's marble ledge and peeked out. The sun was high in the sky, shining on the boys' wing of the orphanage and the statue of the Blessed Virgin Mary at the entrance. Hollyhocks and roses bloomed in the caretaker's garden at the far end of the decrepit playground. I wondered if Never-Never Land smelled like roses. It couldn't smell like Sister Charlie's dorm, a combination of institutional disinfectant, sour milk, and sweaty wool habits whose wearers had never touched deodorant.

I pressed my mouth to the glass pane and studied Mary. "Ma . . . Ma . . . Mother!" I flattened my palm and tapped softly. Then I pushed myself away from the ledge, brought my hands together and gave three soft claps.

Sister Charlie said the movie would be shown in the afternoon.

"When is afternoon?" I mouthed the question and moved cautiously around the other whispering girls. To a child, time is forever, no matter if it's a minute, an hour or a day. To an orphan of Saint Thomas-Saint Vincent Orphan Asylum time was forever infinite, endless.

I tilted my head back and sniffed the air. I worried that someone might dirty their panties, and I tugged several times at my own. If Sister Charlie came into the room and caught a whiff of soiled panties from any of us, we would all pay the price. The offender would suffer the worst of the blows while the others would get a few of their own as a timely reminder.

Yesterday she found a trace of soil in mine.

I sniffed the air again, this time for her smell. No Sister Charlie. She was in her private quarters, and I smiled. Again, I carefully checked my panties. Bending over, my head almost kissing the ground, I pulled up my dress and peered inside. Satisfied, I grinned to no one but myself.

"Afternoon, afternoon, afternoon," I singsonged.

Voices seemed louder than usual today. Whispers magnified.

"Good! Good! Good!" I repeated to myself. "I'm a good girl."

A girl tugged on my arm and whispered in my ear. I pushed her and backed away, then shook my head and said, "No!"

I was only a bad girl for a minute. Without warning, Sister Charlie yanked my hair. Her rough, meaty hand slapped my cheek. "No talking. You will learn to obey the rules!"

I'd broken a Sister Charlie rule.

She jerked me off the floor and I wet my pants. I didn't want to cry. I had to be good, so I could watch *Peter Pan* and not go to Hell.

Sister Charlie's face flushed dark red as she used her favorite form of discipline. She grabbed a fistful of my hair and the hair of the playmate I had shushed then knocked our heads together, causing an eruption of pain followed by brief blackness and speckled, colored spots. I cradled my head and blinked hard. Everything looked distorted.

Sister Charlie snatched me up by my arms and carried me into the stark dormitory lined with white metal cribs. And like a dirty rag, she tossed me into a crib, banging my head on the metal bar along the way. Then she stripped off my dress and panties.

"You bad, dirty, disgusting girl! You soiled your panties again. Bad girls go to Hell!" She picked up her second-favorite form of punishment, the thick, red, wooden paddle.

I scooted to the far side of the crib's bars to escape. Sister Charlie grabbed my leg and held my naked body up in the air. The paddleboard whooshed three times, once on my legs, once on my buttocks, and last on my privates. Then she dropped me onto the mattress. I lay there, trying to hold my breath. Sister Charlie glowered and stomped off, her black robes whipping behind her. Even though I was cold and naked, I didn't dare move. Tears streamed down my face.

A long time went by. I wouldn't see *Peter Pan*.

I rocked my head back and forth, whimpering, "Sister Charlie?"

The shadows on the dingy walls became larger as the sun set. I peeked over the side of the crib to look out the window. The cows were walking into the red barn to be milked. The grass covering the rolling Kentucky hills darkened from rich blue-green to greenish-black. I rubbed my belly. "Hungry. Collywobbles in tummy . . . tummy's hungry. Sister Charlie?"

Maybe Sister Charlie would come and get me. "Sister Charlie, Sister Charlie, Sister Charlie," I singsonged in a whisper.

I tugged on the thin sheet on which I lay, then pulled it up to my mouth and sucked on it for comfort.

I would be good. I would be silent.

One. Two. Three.

Three Blind Mice.

I am three.

I am a very bad girl.

My copious tears made no sound.

Three
Communion

I sat in silence as my husband, Joe, drove me home from the attorney's meeting.

"Well? What was he like?"

"Polite, charming..." I smiled at my rugged, handsome cowboy husband, then closed my eyes and let my head fall back against the seat.

"You okay?" Joe's fingers wrapped around mine like a shield against heartache's thump, and for a brief moment I felt my heart crease, loved, protected; no longer an orphan.

I opened my eyes, met his, and thought, *he still doesn't know.*

Oh, he knew I'd be joining the lawsuit to support my sisters and that I was raised in an orphanage. He knew only that. I'm sure he had suspicions. Still, I had never shared the details of any of the abuses I'd suffered. And, ever gracious, he'd respected my privacy for over seventeen years.

I suddenly felt guilty that I had so easily offered to a stranger what I guarded so closely from my own. I looked down at Joe's hand and I knew I had to talk to him soon. He deserved that.

"It was difficult . . ."

Joe kissed me and I could tell the kiss was balm for past pains I'd suffered and for those I'd yet to receive.

I lapsed into silence.

~~~

Silence. The dozens of nuns, orphans, and the few relatives in the chapel made barely a rustle. I ran my hands over the satin fabric of my Communion dress and waited for Father Lammers to give the signal to approach the altar. I remembered Sister Charlie's earlier warning about keeping the borrowed dress perfect, and I sat on my hands to still them and quiet my mind. I was slowly learning the rules of survival at Saint Thomas.

I was becoming a big girl. How old was I now? Six? Birthdays were not celebrated. And although time was not marked in measures of birthday or celebrations at the orphanage, I'd always felt I possessed a strongly adult sense of time, the way it flew and what all of it meant to hold for me. Still, I needed to remember to ask my sisters the next time Mass ran over. Maybe while passing in the halls, or even better, at breakfast. They always knew.

With age came the promise of survival and strength. Wild Injun, they called me. I took no offense, if the nuns thought me one, I'd act as one. Sometimes I would defy them and refuse to bend when beaten. One of the latest thrashings had taken place on the playground when the nun thought I'd bumped line in the hopscotch line. I did not. I'd been the one bumped. The nun towered over me, hand drawn back, and I found myself once again trying to defend myself with useless, whispering pleas and continued to do so even after two slaps to the face. In the midst of the assault, I remember turning my head, cradling my face to shield the blows.

I caught a glimpse of the road leading out of the orphanage and I snuck a peek upward. The sky was swollen and gray from a quick and sudden spring shower. At the end of the road there was a vibrant rainbow's arch which seemed to pulse like time ticking, then stretch—stretch across and disappear at the entry. Then the sun's rays peeked out showing changes to come. At that moment a strange calm and a sense of control enveloped me. A moment I grabbed and bottled, and one that I found I would reach for again and again during my youth to draw strength from. *One day I'm going to be the rainbow at the end of that road and I will stretch across, disappear, and I will be in charge of my changes.*

I'd turned back to my abuser, raised my chin and gave an ice-cold glare, and it became clear to me that I was nurturing the strength of my spirit with small rebellions. I could outlast them because time was on my side. They knew it and I knew it. And I knew that I'd never be completely broken.

A few weeks prior, I'd passed the big girls when my dorm came in from the playground. Two of the *big* girls bent down and gave me a new word: *dammit.* I'd swished it around my mouth and decided it suited me. It tasted like snake venom, and I liked it. So much so that I gave it freely to my best friend Jenny, and we delighted in its use. It made us feel big-girlish.

I cupped my hands and whispered the word into Jenny's ear. She widened her eyes, grinned and shook her short, strawberry blonde curls. Her blue eyes sparkled as she tried out the word. I covered my mouth to suppress a giggle.

Byrdie Maize, Saint Thomas's only African American, stood nearby. She'd overheard the word, but just smiled sweetly. I saw her and smiled back, after which I gave Jenny a warning look. Jenny smirked and stuck her face in mine. "Dammit."

I shook her tiny shoulders, and finally put my hand over her mouth to keep her from giving it to others. She nipped at my palm, broke free and ran, singsonging, "Dammit, dammit, dammit!"

I almost hollered it after her. Instead, I frowned, turned away and wiped my blood-nipped hand on my dress. Pulling up my sleeve, I hooked it over my shoulder while walking slowly into the building and into Sister Charlie's dorm.

She was waiting for me. I looked into the nun's angry eyes. "You're late. You're dirty," she boomed. She took the hem of my dress, pulled it up and rubbed it hard across my face.

"Dirty Injun!" She gripped my arms and shook me. My teeth chattered. Then she jerked me up by my arm, lifting me easily onto a chair. I heard a snapping sound from my arm and yelped. I blinked back tears and reached to rub the pain only to have her smack my hand.

I made a fist. It hurt. She grabbed my hands and attacked my fingernails with the scissors. "The Devil likes vain, talkative Dirty Injuns, but I'm here to make you pleasing to God." When she finished, I looked and saw they were cut to the quick and bloodied, as always.

"Sister Charlie, my arm hurts bad." I touched my forearm. "Awful bad, Sister Ch — "

She snatched me off the chair and dragged me to Sister Charlotte, the nurse.

Sister Charlotte wiggled my arm, forcing a groan out of me. "Nothing but a greenstick break, if even that," she told Sister Charlie.

All the way back to Sister Charlie's dorm, I kept looking down at my arm, worrying about it turning green, shriveling up, and falling off like a dead twig on a tree.

Sister Charlie jerked my *greenstick arm* and pulled me back onto the chair. A shrill cry escaped my lips.

"Shut your mouth," she spat. She drew back her hand. I put my hand up to my mouth and bit my knuckles to still a sob as she raked her fingers through my hair to untangle it. "You will learn silence." She snatched the scissors and banged a chipped bowl onto my head. "You will also learn humility. And obedience!" Then with a dozen snips she hacked my hair to the level of the bowl's rims — the top of my ears.

I swiped away the tear-damped hairs that stuck to my face, wobbled on the wooden chair, caught my balance, and hugged myself to chase away the worries. This was supposed to be an uplifting day, a momentous day, not a frightening one. Today I would make my First Holy Communion.

"Strip," Sister Charlie ordered. She rapped her bony knuckles on my head and held out her hand while tapping her foot impatiently.

"Yes, Sister Charlie." I hiccupped between sobs.

"And stop that sniveling. You're a big girl now. Big girls don't cry when they're punished. Only bad ones do."

I pulled my brown checked dress carefully up and over my head, winced, and handed it to her. As she prepared to dress me for the Sacrament, I asked, "When will I see my mother?"

She threw the Communion dress on the bed. "You–will–stop–asking–so–many–questions!" She slapped my head and arms and legs at each pause. "This is an important day! You're a big girl now!" She put her face against mine. "And don't you dare soil your panties."

Dead groundhog breath. I clamped my lips tight and held, tried my hardest not to gag, but she saw the look on my face and slapped my head. "Don't you *dare* give me that look!" she said through clenched teeth. "I'll whop it right off."

I didn't doubt it for a minute. Her declared tortures were always delivered. Always.

I flinched. "I'm sorry, Sister Charlie, I—"

She grabbed my greenstick arm and squeezed tightly. "Didn't those wild sisters of yours tell you how to behave?" Her eyes narrowed and the biting words were followed by another hard squeeze to my arm.

Yesterday, the nuns had sent my older sisters, Pamela and Caity, to explain it to me. I really didn't understand the Sacrament. However, my sisters said it was supposed to be special, and I yearned to walk up to the altar with the big girls to receive Communion instead of being left behind in the pew.

Pamela had kneeled down. "Be good," she said, "and don't make Sister Charlie angry."

I always listened to Pamela. She was a ten-year-old *big* girl. She grasped my shoulders lightly and tossed a nervous glance up at Caity. Caity was nine years old, and I listened to her, too. She kept repeating, "Kimmi, don't let the Communion wafer fall off your tongue."

I had no intention of dropping it; I was going to eat it. Pamela fussed with my hair and hugged me goodbye. Caity looked worried. She chewed on her lip, then reached down and pecked my cheek with a small kiss. I reassured her with a bright smile. "Only a small sip of wine, Kimmi, okay?" Caity said. I shook my head no and then nodded yes in agreement.

I was supposed to feel particularly important today. Not like the day two weeks earlier when I'd made my First Confession. I'd shuddered in fear when entering the smelly, claustrophobic confessional booth.

Father Lammers had stepped out of his booth, reached around and impatiently yanked the red velvet curtain closed. The stale reek of ghosted sins hung dismal and threatened to smother me. Turning sharply, engulfed by the sudden darkness, I'd frantically searched for the aged oak kneeler, where I lowered myself down on my knees. Fighting for air, I felt for the wooden screen. When at last I found the wooden peg, I slid it back and was comforted to see another wooden screen, pocked full of tiny holes. It enhanced the sweet slivers of light coming from the priest's side, but the stingy illuminated slices brought a little comfort.

Sweat dripped from my bangs, and my dress molded to my sticky armpits. My voice quivered as I exposed a lifetime's worth of sins to the faceless priest.

"Bless me, Father, for I have sinned." The nuns had drilled the formula into us, using the paddleboard and their hands as incentive. "I gave Regina a mean look and called her Miss Smarty Pants ... Reginee Meanie." I took a deep breath. What else? I'd memorized a long list of sins, terrible things I'd done that would get me sent to Hell as soon as I died. "I said the ... I—" I stopped. Better not use the dammit word in confessional. "Um ... I stayed awake during nap. Uh ..." Oh, I just couldn't tell him about the oatmeal. What if he told Sister Deloris Marie? I couldn't eat it last week, so Caity tossed it in the trash can when no one was looking.

My heart was racing. I didn't want to go to Hell. Words tumbled out. "Oh, uh, um, I didn't eat my oatmeal last week." What was I supposed to say at the end? My hands grew clammy and my heart pounded. Oh yes! "For these and all my sins, I am truly sorry. Name of the Father, Son and Holy Ghost, Amen."

I swallowed hard and crossed myself quickly.

Lingering silence from Father Lammers. I held my breath, waited, expecting my penance: condemnation to blazing Hell. Time clogged and seconds struggled by before he granted my forgiveness and gave me penance: to pray the rosary five times, and to say ten Hail Marys and ten Our Fathers. I released a huge burst of air and literally ran out of the chapel like the wild Injun they professed me to be.

First Holy Communion will be different, I assured myself.

The anticipation of seeing my sisters at the ceremony provided a small, if somewhat confusing, shot of courage. A long time had passed since our initial separation, and I cherished any chance meetings I had with them.

My small stock of courage dwindled in the face of Sister Charlie's anger. I'd been excited, but now my arm hurt and Sister Charlie's behavior was scaring me, and I couldn't fix it—fix Sister Charlie's anger or my soon-to-be greenstick arm.

I wobbled again, as I stood naked on the chair beside my bed. Why was she always angry? I tried to be good. My tears welled and threatened to spill as I fumbled with the white net veil I would wear when I received the Sacrament.

"Oh, my arm, Sister Charlie, my green arm," I moaned softly. She snatched the headdress away and smacked my head. She pressed the attached plastic comb down and dug it into my scalp. I yelped, and Sister Charlie narrowed her eyes.

I reached up to touch the pain. She smacked my hand away, causing me to totter on the wooden chair. She slapped my bare legs again and again, high up on my thighs, where the dress would hide the marks.

In honor of the celebration, I'd received a borrowed Communion outfit. The fancy white dress, veiled headdress, white gloves and shoes added to the mystery of the ceremony.

Crying, shaking, I tried to put on the beautiful white Communion dress over the veiled headdress.

"I said stop that sniveling." Sister Charlie poked my chest with her fingers. "And, Missy, if that dress gets one spot on it or if I see one little rip tonight ..." I winced. Sister Charlie didn't have to finish. She used her hands to remind me. "And I expect good manners! Don't you dare act like a Wild Injun. Your mother is coming for the ceremony and to take you out for a day visit." She pressed her lips tightly together. "God only knows why the woman should be allowed."

I blinked back tears. I was being bad again. Dammit.

"No, Sister, yes, Sister, I'm sorry Sister," I whimpered. "Sister Charlie, I'll take real good care of the dress, mind my manners, I promise." I smoothed down the satin fabric. I didn't see the streaked blood I left behind from my earlier nail clipping. But Sister Charlie would later.

I asked the question uppermost in my mind. "Sister Charlie, do I have to leave my sisters?"

She hiked up the white dress and answered with another smack to my leg. "It's time to go," she said, pulling me off the chair and shoving me ahead of her. I followed her to the chapel's foyer, got in line, and waited until Father Lammers gave us the nod to enter.

And like putting glitter on pigs, the nuns clothed twelve orphaned girls in pretty white dresses, and we walked up to the altar, feeling very grand.

I dared not look around the chapel for my mother, Diane. I didn't know I'd passed right by her while walking to the front pew. I wouldn't have recognized her anyway. I'd only been a baby when Diane fell asleep in bed with a lit cigarette, drunk. The firemen rescued my sisters and me. Again. And after too many years of *again*, the State of Kentucky finally narrowed her eyes, raised her brow, and left us to the charitable care of the Sisters of Charity. There would be occasional, brief visits, but I would not be able to associate the face with the word *mother*, no matter how hard I'd try.

I smelled the cloying incense and tried to hold my breath. The smell always enveloped me, threatening to smother. My stomach churned and I fought back a gag. I knelt on the splintered kneeler, drank from the wine goblet, stuck out my tongue, and received the wafer-thin bread from Father Lammers. "Corpus Christi," he said. I flinched inwardly when he put the wafer on my tongue.

"Amen," I responded and carefully made the sign of the Cross.

I still couldn't comprehend that it was supposed to be the actual body of Christ I was receiving. Bread was bread in my mind, and even a small piece of bread during Mass would bring comfort, perhaps even compensate and counterbalance the nauseating incense smells during Benediction.

The significance behind First Holy Communion meant little else but food to me. I didn't drop the wafer. I savored it; let it melt slowly in my mouth.

The sacramental ceremony went off without a hitch, and I quickly headed back to my dorm for further instruction. I'd been pleased with myself, but my pleasure quickly soured as I thought about meeting my mother.

Sister Charlie dug the veil's plastic comb harder into my scalp. "Be polite. Speak only when spoken to. Place a napkin over the dress when you eat." She spotted the blood on the side of my dress and hissed, "I will be waiting for you when you return."

I let out a small sob, choked it back and blinked away tears. She swatted my legs several more times before walking me down to Mother Superior's office. I sat on the wooden chair in the hollow foyer as I waited to greet my mother. I kept smoothing down the fabric of my dress, smoothing down my nerves with each stroke. When Diane walked in, I looked at her shyly. A quick glimpse showed this mother to be tall and thin except for her tummy area. Her dark brown hair was short and stylish. There was something huge protruding from her belly, as if she'd swallowed a large bouncy ball.

What was she hiding in her tummy?

I couldn't look at the mother—my mother. I wouldn't look at Sister Charlie either. Instead, I stared down at the marble floors, dreading the unfinished business to be seen to after I returned.

"Kim. Kim Michele, come." Diane said. "Come give Mommy a hug. They wouldn't let me see you." She glared at Sister Charlie.

The mother took my hand, and I looked up into her face. In it I saw evils. Her blue eyes were dilated and sunken, her skin blotchy, and the hand holding mine twitched. She smelled funny, like Father Lammers's Communion wine, only stronger. Her words sounded different, sluggish. She must have felt my shudder, because she flushed a little and we walked in silence toward an old car.

The mother tried to make it a special day, but I was so scared. If only I knew why this woman felt so bad to me, so wrong.

For a while I pretended to be the little princess in the Shirley Temple movie I'd seen last week, and imagined that the Communion dress was her beautiful gown and the car was taking her to see the queen of England.

I stole peeks at Diane throughout the day but was given no help with my unanswered questions.

We pulled up to an old Texaco station with rusty gas pumps instead of a palace, and Diane stood me in front of the sign and took a picture of me in the beautiful white Communion dress.

I pretended I was the princess eating supper with the queen when we shared peanut butter sandwiches and a sliver of buttery pound cake for dessert while seated in the back seat of the car.

"Do you and your sisters like school, Kim Michele?"

"Yes, ma'am, sort of, I guess." A cake crumb fell out of my mouth onto a napkin on my lap, and I whispered a relieved dammit that the dress stayed clean.

She rubbed her bouncy-ball tummy. "Are you happy?"

I wondered if she'd eaten too much pound cake and was worried it would pop. I worried that if I told her the truth and got her mad, I'd make the bouncy ball pop. So I said yes.

It was dusk before my mother delivered me back to Saint Thomas's steps. She gave me a brief hug, waved once, got into her car and sped away. I stood a moment and watched until I could no longer see the blue smoke trails from the car's exhaust.

The foyer was dark and deserted. My quiet footsteps echoed down narrow halls as I made my way to my dorm. Sister Charlie was waiting. She grabbed the side of my dress and jerked it. "Look at the blood on that dress! You–filthy–pig! Wash it now!"

I looked down at the dress, then to the dried blood caked on my nails. I gulped air.

She yanked the veil from my head, along with some of my hair. "And take a bath. You stink."

I took as long as I could, rubbing vigorously to erase the blood stains. Then I handed her the cleaned, but still bloodstained dress to dry and walked to my big-girl bed. I trembled and my mouth grew parched. I felt clammy and surreal. Beads of sweat formed on my upper lip and began to trickle down. Licking the salt from my lips, I tasted fear.

The dorm was dark and held an uneasy silence.

Most of the children who occupied the white iron beds were asleep or pretending to be. I climbed into bed and covered myself with the thin sheet. Maybe she'd forget, be too tired. Maybe she'll go away. Go away, go away, Sister Charlie.

"Pigs shouldn't wear white!" Sister Charlie loomed over me, growling. "You're grimy, like the dress you soiled." She punched me in the stomach. Again. The peanut butter and pound cake sloshed in my throat. She grabbed my throat and shook me, her fingers gripping my windpipe like a rope, tightening, tightening. She released me and I fell sideways off the bed. I crossed my arms in front of my face.

She kicked her heavy pointed shoe into my stomach. I pulled myself up to a kneeling stance, clutched my stomach and vomited Diane's celebratory lunch all over the bedclothes.

"You filthy disgusting girl!" She grabbed my hair, lifted me back onto the bed and shoved my face into the mound of undigested peanut butter, cake and bile. She picked up the red paddle and whacked my back and behind until I lost control and urine hissed down my legs and puddled on the sheets. "You're bad. Evil! No better than a *wild Injun!*"

She ripped off my panties and slammed the paddle down on my privates. I screamed into the vomit and inhaled bile and cake and bread. She beat my exposed privates again, then she dropped the board and punched the side of my head. Stars shot through my eyes and my ears rang. She missed once and her hands plowed through vomit.

"Satan's fires won't be hot enough for Wild Injuns!" She wiped her hand over my hair and into my eyes. "You're soiled, impure."

Punch. Then another. After a while I stilled and did nothing to avoid the blows. I simply waited. And then I prayed I would be in heaven soon.

But no, I thought, that wouldn't be right. You go to Hell when you're bad. And I'm bad. Sister Charlie always says so.

I'll go to Hell!

Full panic set in and I made an attempt to rise. She jerked me off the bed and I swayed and fell against her. She caught me by my hair and yanked me upright.

"Clean up this mess and be quiet about it. I have to go to prayers now." Sister Charlie stomped off.

Mustering all my strength, I stood wobbling, darkness threatening. I looked down at my mess—her mess—and blinked hard to focus. My shaky hands grabbed the iron bedpost for support. Every single part of me hurt, swelled. As I slowly bent to strip the bed, I swallowed hard and suppressed a scream. I didn't dare.

I gathered the ragged linens in my hands and headed for the laundry area down the hall, stumbling over the bed sheets. After several attempts to gather the unwieldy mess in my arms I gave up, letting them trail behind me. It took two long, excruciating trips to the laundry room. My tears fell, blending into the waters held by the nicked white porcelain tub, which seemed to fill slower than usual. Through bleary eyes, I looked for the orphans' step stool, as the washing tub was as tall as me.

I tottered on the stool and clung to the side of the tub for strength. A few drops of blood plunked into the water. I touched my tongue to my lip. It was split. My ears rang. My head pounded. My hands shook as I tried to complete the late-night task. I folded in the linens and poured the industrial-strength laundry detergent on top. The pain in my hands was excruciating. They were swollen and red, beginning to bruise where the wooden paddleboard had hit.

I reached in to swish the waterlogged linens. I stopped and let the running water stream over my hands, then cupped water in my hand and let it drip slowly over my swollen arm. I checked to see if it had turned green yet. I moaned weakly and fresh tears of pain matched the flow of water and disappeared in the slow-filling tub.

After a very long time, I put the thin linens through the old wooden wringer and cranked it around and around until I was sure I'd squeezed all the water out. If Sister Charlie found water on the floor in the morning, she'd pour laundry detergent down your throat until you bubbled out vomit.

I'd left water last week.

After hanging the linens as best as my shaking hands allowed, I walked back to my bed. In the darkness, I felt the stares of some of the other children, and I raised my chin slightly as I walked past the little iron beds. I climbed into the cold, bare bed, then painfully curled up into a tight ball and let the darkness relieve my emotions.

I rocked softly and silently mouthed the words of my childish nightly prayer for protection. "Now I lay me down to sleep, I pray the Lord my soul to keep. If I should die before I wake, please give Sister Charlie all my birthday cake."

I listened for a while to the soft hissing of the old water radiator heaters. I thought about the beautiful white Communion dress I'd worn, now stained with blood. Soiled purity. I took comfort in my silent tears, and darkness came quickly.

Four
What color is strength?

2005

I picked up the white skirt and slung the light-green pantsuit across the bed, then sat down and looked at the old Jenny Lind trunk, which I had forged into a nightstand.

What would Emily Post wear to a deposition?

It had been scheduled many months before, giving me plenty of time to prepare. The request came from the attorneys of the Sisters of Charity of Nazareth and the archdiocese of Louisville, Kentucky. It would take place at William McMurry's office. The lawsuit would proceed into its next phase: depositions of all parties.

I sighed and looked at the clock sitting on the trunk. I had less than an hour to get to William's office.

I picked up the brown leather Bible sitting next to the clock and flipped the pages. Small newspaper clippings of obituaries cascaded down, landing in perfect succession—a timeline of final ceremonies. Grandmother, mother and sister. The child of, granddaughter of, daughter of, sister of Kim.

I glanced over to the copied newspaper lying on the bed and stared at the article on William F. McMurry, the great-grandson of a Methodist bishop, son of a judge, and older brother to two sisters, the younger of whom had been molested by a neighbor. I frowned.

Closing the Bible, I picked up one small clipping and ran a finger over it. Words blurred and my hands shook.

My oldest sister, Pamela.

"Who would speak for Pamela?"

I fought to catch a breath. If I didn't go through with this, my dead sister's voice would be silenced forever. No one could speak for Pamela today, tomorrow, or ever, except me. She'd chosen alcohol and drugs as her weapons to fight her childhood monsters, Father Lammers, and the Sisters of Charity. The monsters had won.

Carefully I placed the clipping and my memories back into the Bible. I needed to stay on track, but I already felt I'd jumped off and someone needed to clean up the wreckage. I pressed my fingers to my temples and rubbed. The Tylenol I'd swallowed at six that morning, along with a dose of an anti-anxiety drug, promised no reprieve. I knew the small dose wouldn't help, but I'd learned from my mother and my sister's drug and alcohol addictions the consequences of abuse. And I'd educated myself and heeded the warnings for children of substance abusers. And those warnings said: Steer clear. I used medicines wisely, sparingly and with extreme caution.

I shivered. My hand was on the doorknob. I was about to open the closet where my monsters slept. And I felt five years old again.

I considered the outfits carefully; choosing the green over the white, although I knew the clothes wouldn't mask my fear. The light green pants and matching jacket brightened my green eyes and complemented the blonde highlights in my always-tousled hair. A pink and green silk chemise peeked out of the jacket giving my outfit that perfectly finished look.

I'd thought about pink. It was one of those iffy colors. What did they say about pink? Something about vanity? So many rules to contend with, so complicated. I'd read those books on what colors meant and what season you were supposed to be. Did green mean submissive? Weak? Insecure? What was it?

Damn, why in hell didn't I just wear the black tailored suit? I knew better. Nuns wore black. Black equals power! The nuns' power, the mind games, suppression and guilt they'd inflicted on me had chased me right into adulthood. Their words and actions still overshadowed even the smallest of my daily routines.

I stood up and walked over to the mirror. My face showed fatigue. The impending lawsuit was already wearing on me and it had only begun. Stress and worry had become constant, and the ever-present circles under my eyes attested to it.

I moved back from my reflection and sighed. Joe came up from behind and wrapped me in his strong arms. "Bout ready?"

"Mmm."

"I can stay with you today." He nuzzled my neck. "You don't have to do this alone, you know?"

"No, you've already taken time off to drive me. That's enough, but thanks, luv."

I loved this man and was so thankful for him. I needed his strength, his patience. It seemed to come so naturally to him, and he lived it every day as a police commander.

I tried to speak but couldn't. I wanted to tell him about the childhood abuses, that it wasn't just about the abuse Caity and the others had suffered, but I was concerned about shielding him. I wasn't worried about him judging me. That wasn't his nature. I was worried about always being strong, about the conflicts it could bring on top of his daily work. I'd always fought hard to make sure his home, his sanctuary, was free of conflict.

I knew we were strong. We complemented each other well, even though our temperaments were opposite. I was a Sunday morning preacher's fiery sermon, and Joe was the sweet pause of silence before the Amen. But how would I stay strong and protect my family from this? I stiffened in his arms.

"Joe, what about the press, the backlash from the lawsuit?"

"We'll deal with it." He hugged me tighter.

"But people. The gossip, Joe?"

"Hon, I love you. You're my wife, and that's all I care about. My loyalties are to *you*."

I was silent as I gazed out the car window. Joe chatted as he drove me to the deposition, more to ease my fears, I suspected, than to converse. It was distracting and oddly comforting at the same time. I wasn't sure if I welcomed the chatter or needed silence. Resigned, I took a deep breath. I had given my sister Caity my word, promised my support.

Promises made, promises kept.

I stole a glimpse at my husband, hands relaxed as he steered the car. I reached for his hand to draw on his strength. I squeezed lightly, then released it and reached for the car visor. After inspecting myself for the hundredth time, I snapped the visor mirror back in place, crossed my arms, and looked out the window at the passing bluegrasses of Kentucky.

"Love ya, like salt loves meat," Joe said softly.

"Mmm, love you, like a woman loves chocolate." I gave a small smile, then looked down at the watch that attested to our love. Joe had surprised me with its unique gyro-type, which flipped over to reveal our favorite sentiment engraved on it.

We'd discovered the ancient saying at the annual Corn Island Storytelling festival while dating and had quickly claimed it as our own by reversing a few of the original words; *I love you like meat loves salt.* Sometimes it became ridiculously childish when we'd try to outdo one another, by thinking up clever sayings. I had giggled at Joe's last silly one; *I love you like a dog loves a fire hydrant.*

Years ago, I'd searched endlessly to secretly hire a jeweler to design a pendant in the shape of a saltshaker, with our saying engraved on it for him. We'd laughed like little children that Christmas when we opened our gifts. Unbeknownst to the other, we each had the same idea. Joe wore his necklace proudly under his police uniform, never taking it off. And my watch was a perfect, timeless reminder of our love.

I looked down at my jacket and frowned again at my choice of clothes.

"Joe, this green—"

"You look beautiful, hon."

"I don't want to look beautiful. I want to look strong."

"You are strong."

"Hmph, green." I scowled. "Should have gone with the black. Even whore red would have been better."

It was too late now. No time to change from skins to armor.

"Nun-black would have been better."

Joe chuckled.

"Clothes! I'm tired of obsessing about deposition-day clothes. The nuns have no worries: they squeeze into five yards of black serge, pin on three yards of veil, and they're done for the day."

"Gives them plenty of time to pray for God to enlighten the poor sinner who's taking them to court." Joe gave a devilish grin.

Oh, to Hell with them. I survived too many years of penance, beatings, and their passive-aggressive bullcrap. I can survive eight hours in a room with a Sister of Charity. And I will look damn good doing it. Let's see, mint-green trousers, matching blazer, and the beige pumps with one-inch heel—I just couldn't bring myself to wear the sexy three-inch heels. And oh, I can just hear Mother Superior *tsk tsk* and whisper to Sister Mary Right-hand-man how the world has corrupted me. Just loud enough for me to hear, of course.

I smiled at the pink and green blouse. Hmm, it showed just a hint of cleavage. Bite on that, Sister.

I really needed to feel powerful and strong today, to summon up my yesterdays.

Five
Hard medicine

Death was more powerful than Sister Charlie.

On the fourth day after Sister Charlie's death, her body disappeared from the chapel's altar, and with that disappearance came my ascent to Sister Charlotte's dorm.

I slouched over the school desk, rested my chin on my hand, pencil perched in mouth and stared out the classroom window. I thought about Sister Charlotte, the orphanage's practicing nurse. Except for heavy black shoes, she wore all white. Her flowing white robes and matching sleeves and headdress probably had something to do with medicine, I decided.

Sister Daniel's smarting ruler-whack to my knuckles redirected my attention. I looked down at my schoolwork— the finer points of penmanship that day—but, after a few moments of listening to her monotone voice, I drifted back to the upcoming event: moving into the big girls' dorm.

I stared out the classroom window, smiled and thought about the afternoon. After lunch the girls would go to the boys' side of the orphanage. I loved it there. It was much better than the girls' playground. The boys' playground, the first one built, had swings, horseshoe pits, hopscotch and grassy commons. The girls' playground had been added later. It was a stingy afterthought and reflected just that. The boys' swing set faced the road that led out of the orphanage. There, I'd lose myself for hours, watching and dreaming of what lay beyond.

I barely heard Sister Daniel's dismissal. Silent girls formed single-file and moved out of the chalk-dusted classroom toward the cafeteria. Jenny and I reached the end of the corridor. We leaned our heads together.

"So much is happening, all in one week even!" I whispered.

Jenny grabbed my hand, swung it high and said, "Dammit."

"Dammit," I said with a grin.

"And we don't have to take naps once we move to Sister Charlotte's dorm," Jenny said.

"I despise them." I stuck out my lower lip and blew the scraggly bangs back from my forehead. "In Sister Charlie's dorm, we weren't allowed to lie on our bed for naps. Remember?"

"Yup, I remember all the times we'd go into the washroom and line up on the floors." Jenny widened her eyes. "But no, no ... not in the big girls' dorm."

I'd spent what seemed a lifetime of taking naps on the cold concrete, shivering.

"We are big girls now! And no more naps!" I giggled. We linked hands and swung our arms in a toast.

"Dammit," Jenny affirmed. "A visit to the boys' playground—"

"And a new dorm. Imagine."

Yes, I surely must be a big girl.

At least seven, I thought.

I worried that the governing priest, Father Lammers, would be at the horseshoe pit on the playground today. I thought of him as the wolf. I did not like him and had gifted him and his magic tricks with my *dammits* no less than a thousand times.

He'd wave his big hands, motioning us forward. "Watch the magic bug disappear." He'd grin. Father Lammers loved for the little orphan girls to sit on his lap. Luring us with the promise of magic, he'd pretend to make the large black mole—the bug on his hand—disappear.

Then he'd touch privates. It hurt.

Sometimes Father Lammers lived at the orphanage. Whether it was for an overnight visit or for weeks, the nuns became excited and fussed cheerfully about. Their adoration pleased him, and he held court frequently, basking in their compliments.

Jenny and I walked into the cafeteria and took our assigned seats. We bowed our heads, prayers were said and the small bowl of rice-mixed gruel disappeared into our hungry stomachs. Heavy metal doors swung open, banging loudly, as we raced to the boys' playground.

I stopped, rapid breaths spilling out. My hand reached up, smoothing down my wind-tossed hair. Looking suspiciously around the playground, I smelled the wolf. There was no mistaking the odors of pipe tobacco and alcohol. I spotted him sitting near the horseshoe pit, and he wasn't wearing his Mass clothes. He wore khakis and a brown checked shirt. His brown wavy hair was slicked back. Father Lammers waved. I met his eyes and quickly turned away. Climbing into the swing, I was careful to face the front of the road instead of the pit area.

I'd argued with a freckled redhead named Regina in order to secure the swing. I grabbed the swing's chain and squeezed hard. Regina swung her fist and missed. "Kimmi, give it to me!" She growled and gritted her teeth.

I glared and jerked harder on the metal chain even though it cut into my palm. Then she witched her dirty fingers toward my face. She was bigger than me but I was stronger. Still, I sported a fresh bloodied scratch from the victory. I wiped the blood off my cheek, smiled, and leaned my head against the metal chain.

Feeling secure in the rubber-seated swing, I twisted in circles, winding the chains, tighter and tighter. When I lifted my feet to start the dizzying spin, the low squeaky whines of the metal chains brought forth a lost lullaby. Humming, I felt comfortably forgotten, far away from the pit and Saint Thomas.

Jenny cupped her hands, called my name three times and finally spewed forth the gifted dammit word twice before gaining my attention.

"Hurry, we're supposed to go to Sister Charlotte's dorm now!" she said nervously. She pulled me out of the swing.

Excitement, fear and hope raced through me.

"Later in the week, we'll see a Shirley Temple movie!" I said. "Shirley Temple is my favorite! I'm going to be very good. I just can't miss this movie for the world!"

Jenny bit her lip and nodded.

"Oh, and I really want Sister Charlotte to like me. Do you think she'll like us, Jenny?"

Jenny looked worried.

"The older girls said Sister Charlotte is very mean!" Jenny frowned. "And she makes you take medicine. Ew!"

"I've visited her for medicines, seen her at Mass and other places a lot. She really does look mean." I grimaced.

It had to be so! I thought.

"She keeps a dog in her dorm," Jenny continued. "The other nuns don't like it." She frowned. "And it's mean just like her." She wagged her finger in warning. "We'll get bitten."

Jenny and I retrieved our clothes from Sister Charlie's dorm, and then walked up to Sister Charlotte's second-floor dorm. We went into the hall and lined up with the other girls.

Sister Charlotte's squinty eyes took stock of our late arrival. With a medium frame, white wisps of hair wildly poking out of her wimple, and flint-gray eyes hidden behind spectacles, she did look mean.

Beside her feet stood an obese brown Chihuahua. Both Sister Charlotte and her dog, Beigy, looked as if they might bite at any minute.

I could have shouted with joy when I received my assigned locker. I whispered instead, "Number eight, my favorite number!"

"Six." Jenny smiled.

I unpacked my few belongings: a threadbare nightgown, two pairs of socks, two panties, and my faded pink-checkered dress. I looked down at my tattered brown loafers and couldn't decide if I should toss them. They really weren't needed in Sister Charlotte's dorm, especially in winter. For some strange reason, Sister Charlotte preferred her charges to go outside barefoot in the winter. She was adamant about this and had even persuaded some of the other nuns to make their girls do the same. Our little feet turned blue as we played upon the crunchy ice and snow.

Something to do with medicine, I'd assumed. I placed the shoes in the very back of the locker and arranged and rearranged my possessions a half-dozen times before I was satisfied.

Sister Charlotte called out, "Bed assignments."

We lined up single-file and followed her into our sleeping quarters. The large boxy dorm held twenty-five white metal beds, ten were lined up along the walls on each side with long narrow windows above each. The rest of the narrow beds were lined in rows, filling the center. The second-story windows were barren, letting us see the world outside.

Sister Charlotte stopped, called out a name, and pointed a girl to her bed. My bed faced the front of the dorm, the first bed beyond the wide entryway into the sleeping area.

"Line up, girls!" Sister Charlotte commanded. With cool detachment, the old nun looked over her new charges. She withdrew a spoon and green jar from the folds of her habit. Each of us opened our mouths to receive a heaping spoonful of mentholated salve. I shuddered at the taste and despite my gag reflex, I got it down. This would be the nightly pattern while under her care.

Beigy growled and bared his stained yellow teeth. There was no getting around the grouchy old dog's bold warning. To get to my locker and into the washroom, I had to pass by him. His feeding area all but barred the entry door. The orphans would shove each other toward the plump Chihuahua, to provoke him further.

I never understood why Sister Charlotte wouldn't feed her dog in private and away from the early morning stampede of eighteen little girls. Later in life, I thought it one of those twisted obsessions that only twisted people can understand.

One morning I inched my way along the narrow passage. Regina pushed me toward the snarling dog and Beigy nabbed my ankle with a piercing bite. I punched Regina in the stomach and then saw a sour-faced Sister Charlotte glare down at me.

I'd been bad again. You go to Hell when you're bad.

Sister Charlotte went to her private quarters and returned with an amber medicine bottle. She crooked her finger, signaling me to come forward, then poured the clear liquid into a spoon. I opened my mouth and choked on its bitterness. She pointed to my bed and I went without comment. Restless, I tossed and turned and looked around the empty dorm in despair. I had really wanted to see that Shirley Temple movie. "Dammit, dammit, dammit!" I stormed.

Bitter tears flooded my eyes. I pounded my fists upon the bed. The liquid Sister Charlotte had just given me left a funny taste in my mouth. I kept trying to swallow it back. I needed to spit but I didn't dare.

Why didn't Sister Charlotte move Beigy's feeding area? My ankle still stung from the bite. I bent over, blew hard and fanned my ankle several times. Usually Beigy's growl was worse than his bite. I was finding the same held true for his mistress as well. The medicine hurt less than words or fists.

Oh, I couldn't wait to hear about the Shirley Temple movie! Jenny would tell me everything, and it would be just like being there.

Drowsy from the drug, I lay there contemplating images from the last Shirley Temple movie and my eyelids grew heavy. My tongue thickened and my voice slurred as I struggled to whisper my nightly prayer. And with the aid of Sister Charlotte's specialty, angry, silent tears faded into sleep.

Six

And the righteous shall rule

2005

"Don't worry hon, these types of cases are McMurry's specialty."

I nodded in agreement as I stopped in front of the elevator door. Joe hooked his thumb under my chin and kissed me softly. His caress, an unspoken word of love, briefly erased my fears.

"I'll call you when it's over." I looked down at my watch. "It'll be at least eight hours." I offered a small, brave smile, then stepped into the elevator. My courage faded.

My hands shook slightly as I paused to study the gold lettering on the glass door: William F. McMurry, Attorney at Law. I lowered my head to the glass door, to draw strength and to rationalize.

"I'm strong," I whispered. I waited for spiritual affirmation, for courage, but none came. Only silence, like the silence of a nightmare stuck perpetually in slow motion, before the frozen scream breaks loose. Disgusted by my weakness, I raised my head and stepped back from the door. I looked down at my palms, rubbed the cold dampness against my green jacket, and flexed my fingers to still the shake. I took a deep, calming breath, then another, reached for the brass knob and slowly opened the door.

William's assistant attorney was leaning on the secretary's desk, waiting. She would be presiding over my deposition given in my lawsuit to the Sisters of Charity of Nazareth's organization and the Louisville, Kentucky archdiocese's attorneys. She ushered me in. Speaking quietly, she quickly gave me small details as to how the deposition would play out then led me into William's conference room. She couldn't do all that much to help me once the questions got started, she said, but if things got real bad she might think of something.

Five strangers wearing dark clothes stood up from the large conference table, and handshakes were exchanged.

Nun-black, I grimaced. Again, I cursed my clothing decision. My throat tightened, and I suddenly felt seven years old—like the seven-year-old orphan I'd been, was, would always be.

A formal legal intro for the court reporter, then the Sisters of Charity's attorney threw the first punch. "I'll be asking you some questions today." she began.

I was sure they could hear, even see, my heartbeat.

"I'm not trying to ask anything that's gonna confuse or trick you. If I ask you a question that confuses you, let me know and I'll rephrase it and ask it in a different way. Okay?"

I nodded and heard someone say to answer out loud.

"Can you state you name for the record…?"

I looked over to the nun, seriously gave thought to answering, Wild Injun, instead chose *obedience* and answered correctly, not snidely with a simple "yes", but my whole name.

Papers shuffled then I heard the word *orphanage*.

They were asking about the orphanage. I leaned in, felt my forehead knot and knit and tried to focus on words instead of fear.

"Orphanage?" I asked.

Details of abuse. They wanted details.

It was painful to describe the architecture of Saint Thomas's building without having a panic attack that would have me running to the bathroom to relieve my nervous stomach. I didn't want to think about what my body's response would be when I described the horrors inside those tall, suffocating brick walls.

"The abuses?" asked the opposing attorney.

Evil, I thought. Describe evil? That your precious priest and brides of Christ who ran the orphanage were evil? With no one to account to, who would care? Who would know?

Someone asked for a small break to fix the video and I leaned back in the seat and released a small burst of air.

Just a little over three hours, and I doubted my strength. As it ground on, the deposition felt more like a police interrogation. I was getting defensive when I had hoped to remain cool and calm, but now I was about to lose it, and I never lost it.

I knew I'd already crossed the line from civility to hostility, and I knew I was damn close to stumbling. And that's exactly what they wanted, exactly what I'd been told not to let happen.

"The nuns used to force-feed us. I couldn't stomach the almost daily oatmeal gruel that they dished out." *What a turkey buzzard wouldn't even touch.* I reached up to tuck back my hair, but quickly placed my hand back into my lap when I felt its shake.

"I couldn't keep the food down. It was horrible." As soon as I said this, I felt a tinge of guilt for complaining about food when so many in the world went hungry.

"So you didn't like the food?" the attorney asked.

The nun smirked, I cringed and once again I felt distracted. A lifetime of smirks. Well, why should it be any different now? Did they teach that at nun school, Smirks 101: one hundred and one ways to smirk effectively? Still, this nun didn't look or act like a nun from my past.

Long gone were the starched habits. Everyday street clothes had long since replaced them. In passing, one would guess this new breed of nun to be someone's kindly grandmother. I studied her face. Gentle, sweet. I winced. How can I punish such? I scanned my memory for past images of my sisters for strength.

My eyes narrowed. I wasn't falling for the grandmother act. The layers were slowly being peeled, exposing threaded secrets hidden beneath the habit.

The nun leaned over and whispered to the male attorney and I shuddered. I shot her a warning look. She looked smug and comfortable. Too comfortable. I shifted uneasily in my chair, gripped the armrests and waited.

Several yawns from the deposers. Was it boredom I was sensing? Smug indifference? And that attitude began to change mine, gave me calm for one small moment. I touched my wrist and felt the rough textured beads of my cherished scarab bracelet. One tiny comfort.

It was true that time and the Statute of Limitations were against me and the other former orphans involved in the legal proceedings, but damned if I cared at this point. The Church had been in charge of my emotions and my daily existence for too long.

I realized I was holding my breath and slowly exhaled.

Seated at the end of the conference table was a young male attorney. The Sisters of Charity of Nazareth had sent one female attorney to represent their organization, and the Church had sent one male to represent the archdiocese of Louisville, Kentucky.

The male attorney yawned again. The nun and her female attorney mimicked the yawns. It distracted and caused me to lose focus.

I sighed and looked to the clock then back to the attorneys for the second time in fifteen minutes. The deposition was sapping my energy. Again I glanced at the clock, then thankfully, someone called for a short break.

I hurried to the ladies' room. I looked at the reflection in the mirror that confirmed my fatigue. Scooping handfuls of cold water, I splashed my face and prayed for renewed force and control. The mirror, not my best friend at that moment, reflected my fear and fatigue.

I looked at my watch as I headed back to the conference room. How would I ever endure eight to nine hours cooped up with the Church's clergy and its representatives?

The court reporter gave me a friendly smile as we passed in the hall. "Pretty shade of green. Where did you find it?"

"Thank you," I responded weakly, "but I should've worn black."

Settling back in my seat, I looked at the attorneys with guarded suspicion and gave my best smirk to the nun. And the deposing continued.

The male attorney approached a subject that was off limits. "Where do your children go to school?"

A cold fear clutched my heart, as I remembered their previous visit to my child's school. They had been digging for information on my family. *My* children, *my* family, my internal voiced screamed. Instead I answered, "Is this relevant to my childhood or this case?"

My attorney leaned over and gently informed me that I would need to answer.

Unhappily, I gave the information.

"How long have you been a member of your current parish?"

"Since my child started kindergarten there." I shrugged. "We'd only attended Mass while our child was in elementary and middle school." We became involved, as most other parents did. "My daughter is in high school now."

"But you are involved with the parish?"

The female attorney piped in. "You've contributed your time and finances to the parish, haven't you?" She looked down at her paper. "And you've worked on fund-raising committees. Do you plan to continue doing fund-raising at your daughter's high school — the Church?"

"For the school. I've helped raise monies for the school. But I keep my distance from the Church."

"So you no longer attend your parish? Why did you leave?"

Impatience crossed my face as I looked to the attorneys.

Who wears the face of God? I wanted to scream.

Instead I chose my trusted ally, silence. How could I ever explain the irrational thoughts? That to be anywhere near a

Catholic Church brought on sweaty palms and crippling anxieties. More importantly, I wasn't about to expose my weakness to my closet monsters.

"Well, let's see," I quipped. "Maybe I left because the priest left to marry the eighth grade religion teacher, or perhaps I just didn't care for the new replacement priest, or could it be I got bored of playing Church politics? And I grew tired of raising monies for a parish that unnecessarily incurs debt . . . The new priest received a big house instead of the former priest's condo. And the parish built a new church, supposedly bigger for the growing community, yet after it was built, it held fewer pews. Lot of Church politics. So I feel."

A clearing of throats followed a pause of silence as the attorneys directed their glances downward. I looked at my watch. It was past lunchtime. Fidgeting, I caught myself and tucked one hand back under my bottom.

Mentally, I reached up to touch a tear and found none. Someone had already stolen them. Again.

They asked about Father Lammers. Lots of questions regarding his private quarters; was there a TV in there, a bed, lights? My stomach knotted up as I tried to concentrate.

I pulled out bits and pieces, finding I couldn't bring myself to speak in-depth about it. It was going to take anger, rage on my part to provide the details. Right now my emotions flip-flopped, and I worried my responses would sound more like rubber soles on concrete than sense. It was anguishing. I had not found a balance between crippling rage and forgiveness.

Forgiveness. *Forgiveness?* How do you give forgiveness to those who do not ask ...? Offer forgiveness to those who don't think they need? Sister Charlie, Sister Deloris Marie, Father Lammers, all the rest – they lived and died secure in their righteousness.

"Okay," the attorney said, "its 12:30, so we're gonna take a break for lunch."

My mind raced with unspoken questions of my own as the microphone was removed from my jacket.

"I'm hungry." The male attorney grinned, leaned back in his chair.

My attorney looked at me and raised a questioning brow. I felt the small protests of my own empty stomach, the lifelong familiar I'd grown accustomed to. I could easily make it through the eight-hour deposition without food, a self-discipline rooted in childhood. I studied the grinning attorney, then glanced down at my watch.

"I'm not hungry. I want to continue."

Seven
Oatmeal tears

My stomach was eating itself. I'd felt the gnawing for seven years. I was always hungry, yet I dreaded mealtime. I walked into the cafeteria and saw two girls standing near the far concrete wall, and I winced. I knew they'd been caught talking in the cafeteria. Their cheeks were ballooned with a huge mouthful of rusty well water. Water holding was the habitual punishment for their offense. One girl swallowed her water and then the other spewed it out, spraying water everywhere. Sister Deloris Marie slapped the girls' faces and poured more water from the metal pitcher into their mouths. "You'll hold it till I instruct otherwise. It'll teach you silence."

I looked away, knowing the persecution would last a lifetime. They would lose their whole mealtime trying to complete the nun's cruel task. I was terrified of the nun in charge of the cafeteria. Sister Deloris Marie was a giant, huge in every way. Beefy hands and beefy body. Her habitual roars and explosive temper struck panic and fear in all. And she didn't hesitate to dish out punishment with swift physical violence.

"Knees to the Devil!" I heard the nun holler. I turned to see a big girl tumble out of her seat, drop quickly to her knees on concrete and begin to pray out loud.

"Point those knees to Satan so Heaven can see you for the sinner you are. Don't move until you can feel the fires of Hell," she bellowed.

I instinctively knotted up, scrunched my shoulders hoping this would hide my visibility. 'Feeling the fires of Hell' meant praying through the entire meal and an hour after the cafeteria emptied. Not to mention the fires in cramped, aching knees when you tried to stand afterwards.

I hurried over to the rows of long wooden tables, hard plastic and metal chairs. I saw my sisters and my eyes waved a smile.

Morning meals consisted of glasses of cloudy water, some form of thick gruel or a cold wheat mix. On occasion, the breakfast meal would bring a welcome change: cold dried toast, which I preferred and prayed for on a daily basis.

Evening meals didn't stray far from the morning meals, where gruel mixes of rice with a hint of cream, and perhaps a sparse sprinkle of raw sugar, were offered.

Breakfast was insufferable. Though not really a finicky eater, I couldn't stomach the oatmeal gruel which showed up much too often. An occasional interruption in the schedule would find me eating with my sisters and it gave me much joy. Oatmeal would automatically mar the occasion. I could smell its putrid odor a mile away. The stench was like regurgitated cow-wasted straw. I would really try hard to be brave, but in the end I could never follow through. Oatmeal was my biggest weakness, my biggest fear.

The accompanying glass of sulphurous well water with its brimstone stench told me that oatmeal must be Satan's favorite food. And I was having breakfast with Satan this morning.

Tears threatened. My stomach protested with angry flips and I hissed out my *dammits* as I smelled the bile of cooked oats. Stained from decades of use, the indestructible tan bowls matched the thick-pasted gruel inside, and I winced as my suspicions were confirmed.

The Oatmeal Tears, as my sisters often referred to the meal, soon appeared. I gagged several times and swallowed back a bulge of bile. Pulling up a seat next to Caity, my lips quivered as I pleaded, whined and begged. Much to my relief, Caity would sometimes quickly and slyly eat my oatmeal and silence my tears.

Today was not a sometimes day.

"Dammit." I choked on the word and spit it out. Pamela tapped my shoulder and gave me a stern look. In the past, to avoid the nuns' wrath, my older sisters would try everything, from putting toast, water, and even sugar, when available, into the oatmeal for me.

My sisters whispered and looked over to the ageless oak sugar bucket. It stood tauntingly to the far side of the hall. Its use was forbidden unless a nun felt unusually charitable, a rare occasion. The sugar was only doled out under the nun's watchful eye as a stingy tease to mask the tasteless institutional food.

Caity shook her head and mouthed "No" to Pamela.

I let out a sob, bowed my head and joined in the Morning Prayer. Tucking one shaky hand under my bottom, I rested my eating hand slightly on the table as rules directed.

Caity poured a splash of water into my oatmeal, mixed it and whispered a warning. "Eat." I glared at the bowl then back to Caity. She nudged me and put the spoon in my hand. It was useless. I took the spoon, put it up to my mouth, gagged and spit. Caity gave me a look of disgust, took my napkin and wiped my chin. I put the spoon into my mouth, gagged again, then vomited into the bowl. Caity reached over, slapped my back and I choked, struggling for breath. Tears streamed down my face as I clutched my throat. Her eyes grew wide and she shook me. I gasped, finally caught a breath, and spewed out the rest of the clogged mix.

Sister Deloris Marie appeared, fisted her hand and knocked Caity to the floor. The nun moved swiftly to deliver my punishment. Drawing back her arm, she backhanded me across my face. I dropped my spoon, reached up to my face and felt warm oozing blood. The nun looked at my face, then at her hand, and saw the ice pick she'd been using in the kitchen. She dropped it on the table.

The strike had landed near my left eye. I lowered my head and blood spilled into my eye and dripped into the bowl. The nun grabbed my hair and yanked back. I yelped as sharp pain pierced my neck.

Sister Jean, Sister Camilla, and Sister Deloris Marie huddled nearby.

"Needs stitches."

"Might lead to blindness."

"Send for a doctor."

Sister Jean grabbed my arm and ushered me upstairs to Sister Charlotte's dorm.

"Hold still," she said, wiping away the blood with a cold, wet cloth.

I squirmed, but didn't whimper. I didn't want to get hit again.

"I said, hold still, Miss!" She gave me a shake. Then she squeezed the skin above my eye and stuck it together with something cold. It stabbed my already sore skin and I started to cry.

"There. I put a butterfly clip on it. Stop crying or I'll give you something to cry about."

She turned me around and shoved me out the door. "Go back to the cafeteria immediately. You'll be perfectly fine."

Sister Deloris Marie was waiting with a rag in her hand. She scowled and threw the rag at my face.

"Clean up your mess."

Getting on all fours, my clumsy hands waded deep into the metal wash bucket to rinse the washrag. The industrial-strength bleach water stung my eyes and assaulted my nostrils. After several hours of scrubbing, I stood and walked over to Sister Deloris Marie. Lifting my hands, she inspected them, not the floors. They were not raisined to suit, nor red and raw with blood from the harsh chemicals and scrubbing. An unwritten badge of how hard you worked.

She raised a steel spatula then bared her brown, stained horse teeth in a smirk. "I–don't–see–any–blood–yet, Missy." She struck my knuckles with each break of her words.

Sister Jean and Sister Camilla laughed.

I lowered myself back down to the concrete floor and scrubbed, only interrupting to rub my painful eye. My bleach-watered hands only intensified the pain.

What if I go blind? Or worse, get an infection and die?

The older girls in the kitchen clattered the breakfast dishes as they cleaned them.

Despite the stabbing pain, I grinned. No oatmeal for me today. I finished the floors, stood up and admired my hands. "Raw, bloody, just the way she likes 'em," I whispered. I'd earned my badge and I smiled as I walked toward Sister Deloris Marie.

By some miracle, the wound did not get infected, and my sight remained. I would carry only a small but noticeable physical scar for the rest of my life.

Eight
Witches and werewolves, oh my

I knelt on the concrete floor in the quiet bathroom stall, cradled the toilet, and threw up the last of the oatmeal that Sister Deloris Marie had rammed down my throat during breakfast. I touched my tender lips. It had felt like she was ripping them off with each cram of the spoon.

I heard the dayroom buzzing with anticipation: Father Clay was coming tonight.

I licked my swollen mouth and walked away from the noise, instead heading into my dorm. The wind whistled in between the cracks of wood and ill-fitted glass. I walked over to the tall narrow windows and watched the arrival of dusk heralded by God's colorful painting of the sky. Trying to push the forthcoming visitor out of my mind, I studied God's little every-day masterpiece.

I contemplated the autumn leaves twirling before me. How I wished that the wind would sweep me up and take me far from Saint Thomas.

I leaned closer to cold glass and peered sideways out into the distance. To my left, enclosed by the dusk's quiet, sat the old red dairy barn surrounded by open meadows. To my right stood the forest, deep and dark with its own secrets. Beyond, the hills. The rolling, rolling, and more rolling hills of Kentucky.

I shuddered. I was seven years old, nowhere, forgotten, living in constant fear, surrounded by hate and cruelty I didn't comprehend, where the only golden things in my life were the precious brief solitudes of sleep.

I wished I could fix it. Fix me. I was changing somehow. I felt my soul preparing for storms, while winds whipped at my spirit, like the strong breath of the autumn twists scattering leaves before me.

It seemed it was getting harder to accept and endure the asylum. I felt like Shirley Temple, trying to escape in *The Little Princess* movie. I longed to escape the physical and emotional madness of Saint Thomas. I pressed my face against the pane of glass and searched the horizon. Escape, but to where?

I heard masculine laughter in the background. Father Clay had arrived. Father Clay was a young priest, a handsome man who had started coming to the orphanage a year ago. Gifted with creative storytelling, he would tell us vivid, sometimes gory tales, rife with graveyards, bloody bones and hauntings.

I didn't like the stories one bit. I already lived a scary story, frightened enough without more.

I couldn't feign sickness or fear, or leave at his story telling time. "But Sister, I, uhm, need to wash linens, I, ah, didn't finish my homework."

"Father Clay has come a long way to entertain you and if you disrespect him, you'll be doing more than linens and homework," Sister Charlotte warned.

I entered the crowded dayroom to see the other girls sitting Indian-style on the concrete floor. They huddled around the tall priest, who sat on a small wooden chair. Dreading the upcoming tale, I sucked in a huge breath, seated myself on the floor and concentrated on blocking Father Clay's words. For an hour I kept my mind scrupulously clear of the priest's bloody tales.

I studied my nails, cut to the quick and bloody again this week. I rubbed and rubbed, then blew on them to stop the stinging. I examined the ghost poo growing on my dress. Rolling the lint into tiny lumps, I flicked the balls into air. Then I ran my fingers over the concrete wall behind me and peeled off flecks of gray paint. Silently, I hummed "Dixie Anna," a song from the latest Shirley Temple movie. By the time he was done, I was exhausted from my mental exercise and returned to my dorm with the other girls, more than ready to fall into bed.

I'd fallen fast asleep but was now wide awake and my heart raced. Sweat dripped, tickling my body. I was frozen with fear. I squinted and could barely make out the long dark hall straight ahead of me, with the wide swinging doors at its end. I couldn't see the closed wooden door directly to the right of the entryway, but I knew it was there. It was Sister Charlotte's private quarters.

I'd been holding my breath, and I released a huge burst of air. I pulled the thin cover closer to my body.

There had been an evil witch out in the hall and she had walked toward my bed. I had seen her wild, frazzled blonde hair and chilling green eyes coming toward me. I saw the blood dripping from her eyes, smelled its copper. And I could still hear her slow footsteps. The witch lurked, waited.

I needed to decide which was worse: fear of that thing, or fear of waking Sister Charlotte. The witch would surely kill me, while I'd suffer only the discipline of yucky medicines from Sister Charlotte.

The footsteps grew closer and louder. I clenched my teeth and with forged courage I jumped out of the bed. With my chest thumping wildly, I knocked timidly upon Sister Charlotte's door. Moving close to the door, I pressed my body to wood. Listening. Waiting. The door cracked open. I fell against Sister Charlotte, straightened myself and stared up at the nun.

I was shocked to see her unruly white hair and pink flowered night robe. Never had I seen a nun out of her habit before, much less her full hair exposed. My jaw dropped. I lowered my gaze.

"Sister, there's a witch!" I looked over my shoulder and pointed to the dark hallway.

"Can't you hear the footsteps getting closer, Sister Charlotte? Sister — "

"Hush." She pulled me into her quarters.

The room was small, with white shelves that hung high above a long, narrow, white iron bed and matching nightstand. A small writing table and chair stood near a lone concrete wall.

Largely obtrusive, a green metal and glass apothecary cabinet consumed the opposite wall. Standing alone, it was ominously filled with gauzes, glass jars of colored pills, amber bottles of Mercurochrome, colorless liquids, needles and suspicious-looking crude medical instruments. I shuddered.

Scattered religious pictures hung crooked on the walls. A small milk-glass lamp sat on the nearby writing table, casting a warm and inviting glow about the room. On the floor, beside Sister Charlotte's bed, Beigy slept on a worn but cozy blue faded rug.

I looked wistfully at the rug, then at the contented dog which lay upon it. What came out of my mouth next shocked even me.

"Can I sleep on the rug too, Sister Charlotte, just till the witch is gone? Please, Sister Charlotte?"

"It was only a dream."

"Please, Sister, I saw her, the witch." I ran my fingers over my eyes and traced them down my face. "She has bloody eyes."

She shook her head. "Quiet down, and go back to bed." She grabbed my shoulders, gave a little shake.

"No, Sister, please. Sister Charlotte?"

She pointed to the door. "Miss." Her mouth tightened.

Speaking quickly, I assured her. "I won't be a bother, and I'll share it fair with Beigy. I won't bother him either. Please, please, Sister Charlotte."

Tears spilled as I reduced myself to quiet begging. "I promise to be quiet and I won't bother Beigy, please Sister Charlotte? Please? I—"

"ENOUGH!" She walked over to her apothecary cabinet and took out a cobalt bottle of medicine.

I opened my mouth wide to receive the large tablespoon of liquid and swallowed. She sat the bottle firmly on her writing table, pushed me outside her door and shut it tight behind me.

Wild with fright, I lowered myself to the floor. I chewed on my knuckles and listened for noises. Silence. The footsteps had ceased. I curled up into a tight ball next to Sister Charlotte's door, as close as possible. With one hand on my mouth and the other touching the door, I forced myself to try not to breathe or move, so I wouldn't attract the lurking witch.

I woke to the nudging of a heavy black-toed shoe. Jumping up, I met the inquisitive glare of Sister Charlotte. Her pointing finger directed me back to my bed. The metal coil springs squeaked and moaned, interrupting the early morning silence. It was still too early to get up, so I lay awake, fearing an expected punishment from Sister Charlotte, and fearing even more the witch that would come again tonight.

In the late afternoon I played outdoors. Deborah, one of the *big* girls approached me.

"Sister Charlotte is looking for you, Kimmi. She's in her dorm waiting. You'd better get." She gave me a shove when I just stood and stared at her. "Scat!"

I'd been racing Regina on the playground and was so intent on winning each race that I'd forgotten my nightmare. I made my way slowly across the playground and stalled for time by stopping along the way. I found a patch of clover and latched the stems together to make a necklace. I practiced my skills of shooting with the tall foxtail grasses, by looping the thin, green blades of grass in a circle around the base of the foxtail and aiming high.

I stood and stared up at the brown bricks of the three-story building, and wiped my face with the hem of my dress. Taking a deep breath of country air, then another, I grabbed the knob of the heavy metal door and pulled.

A burst of hot, stale air mixed with disinfectants hit me in the face. The heat from the early autumn day had me flushed, and the sweat had my chopped blonde hair sticking up like an old scorched scarecrow. As I made my way toward my dorm, I held my hands clamped tight to the sides of my head trying to flatten down my hair.

It didn't help.

A shoulder lay exposed because of the poor fit of my checked dress. I pulled it up twice, then gave up. Clamminess took over my body. I sucked in a huge breath and crossed my arms.

Sister Charlotte was waiting. She crooked her finger and wiggled it back and forth. I took two small steps forward and followed. She led me to a rusty tin two-gallon bucket, which stood outside the dorm. It was about twenty feet from my bed.

She showed me that the bucket was about a quarter full of water. Then she pointed to the ceiling, directing me to look. "See? The root of your dream." I looked up expecting to see a witch wrapped in tree roots, instead saw a brown, water-stained ceiling. Old leaks had emptied into the bucket.

"The footsteps you thought you heard last night were the mere sounds of water dripping on metal," she said. "The darkness had cloaked the bucket, preventing you from seeing it. I simply removed the bucket before dawn."

"Oh?"

I stared at the ceiling. Pieces of wet brown plaster hung down like icicles clinging to a muddied cow's teat after an ice storm.

She grabbed my chin, "A dream." Then she grasped my shoulders and turned me around to face the dorm, "Select another bed," she said flatly, her voice as dry as yesterday's burnt toast.

"Oh, uhm, oh."

I chewed on my lower lip and looked up at the old nun suspiciously. Her face showed no emotion, but at that moment an unspoken relationship developed. A crumb of kindness had been extended.

I looked over the dorm and its identical white metal beds, before she could change her mind. I settled for the last bed under the window, in the very back of the dorm beside the stairwell door. Its location offered relief, being the nearest to the exit.

I looked over my shoulder several times as I smoothed out the bedspread. "The witch won't get me here," I whispered. I glanced up at the exit sign's soft red glow, and breathed a small sigh of relief.

My somewhat satisfied mind had no way to know, to imagine, to fear that the bed I'd picked would bring a living nightmare more sinister than any witch.

Nine
The cloak of darkness hides the most evil deeds

Sister Charlotte's medicine kept the witch away, but one night she made me drink a different medicine before bed. Thick and bitter, the taste made me gag, and she gave me twice the amount she usually did with her elixirs. She'd said, "Another dose, Miss, you'll soon be eight."

Someone roughly shook me. My sleep-filled eyes struggled to focus on the imposing black form bent over my bed. I staggered to my feet and squinted. It was dark and silent in the dorm. The only sign of light was the glow of the exit sign hanging above the stairwell door next to my bed.

I shivered, covered one bare foot over the other, swayed and bumped against the nun. She grasped my shoulder and gave a shake. I stumbled again, caught myself by grabbing the marble window ledge, straightened and followed the unknown nun in silence to the exit. The nun grabbed my arm and we went out the metal door into the unlighted stairwell. Pausing before the first step, the nun retrieved a tapered beeswax candle from within her robe, lit it, and placed it in its small cast-iron holder.

I'd never seen this nun before. She was not from the boys' dorm.

"Sister? Are you from the visiting quarters? Where—?" My words were slow-moving.

She turned and placed her free hand over my mouth. "Shush."

I flinched as her rough hand squeezed hard, then released my mouth. Continuing down two flights of cold concrete stairs, the nun opened the heavy metal door to enter the first floor hall and we headed toward the main entrance. I found myself standing in front of Father Lammers's private quarters, concealed by a thick wooden door.

I passed it every day on my way to the cafeteria. On rare occasions, it would be open, allowing me to catch a glimpse into a much different world from my own. I'd see a long, polished dining table with tapestry-cushioned chairs. The happy chatter of nuns and the tinkling of silver on china could be heard floating freely about. I'd catch the scent of fresh eggs and chops, or recognize the alluring aroma of bacon and ham. But what I'd always noted and found fascinating were the grapefruit halves, each with a cherry in its center that always accompanied each setting. They looked so beautiful. The strong aroma of fresh-brewed coffee mingled with scented herb teas filled the air and wafted out into the hall, leaving me both dizzy and starved. Father Lammers would be seated at the head of the table, much like a king holding court.

The mysterious nun pushed me into the room and shut the door behind me. My eyes grew wide as I adjusted to the surroundings. In the dim light I made out the dining table, set with pretty glass dishes in preparation for the next morning's meal. The room was warm and stuffy, unlike the cold dorm I'd just left behind. It smelled of alcohol and stale pipe tobacco.

My bare feet sank into a thick rug. A large, carved desk was covered in paperwork and a bottle of wine sat on its center. Beside the wine was a stack of new Holy Cards, which were piled in a flowered clear-glass bowl. Colorful pictures of Catholic saints and religious icons adorned the cards. I spied them and turned abruptly away. They were given to the orphans as rare rewards. Coveted for their illustrated beauty, we'd trade, bribe, borrow, or steal them from each other.

Father Lammers sat to the side of the desk in a well-worn, leather wing-back chair. He motioned for me to come forward. I wavered, still groggy from Sister Charlotte's medicine, then took a small step toward him.

He was wearing a white t-shirt and khaki pants. The priest was a tall man of forty-odd years, with a trim build. His thick brown hair was styled in a conservative duck's ass attempt—the style the big girls referred to. Although I could see no duck or donkey, I could smell the oily, sweet cloying smell of Brylcreem. I choked back a gag from the smells of machine oil and medicinal tang, which blended with tobacco and alcohol.

I swayed a little and shifted uncomfortably as Father Lammers stared at me. He picked up his pipe, dipped into the tin of Borkum Riff, then took a pinch and packed it. Lighting the pipe while he puffed, he let the smoke curl around his mouth. Content after a few more puffs, he knocked the ashes out by tapping the pipe against his shoe. He laid the pipe on a tray's crook, then picked up a goblet filled with wine.

I looked down, saw old ash burns on the carpet then directed my attention to the large mole on his hand. He gestured to me to come closer. I hesitated and looked back to the door. My skin crawled as his eyes snaked over me. I moved two small steps forward.

"Pick out a Holy Card, Kim," he whispered.

I hesitated, and he pointed to his desk. I blinked hard to focus, reached in the crystal bowl and randomly withdrew one. I held it up to him, swayed slightly, then stumbled forward. My mind was foggy. I took two careful steps back and folded my arms over my chest.

"Kim."

I swallowed hard. Silence.

His huge hand motioned again for me to come forward. My feet felt leaden. Then, with hesitating obedience, I came to stand before him. I hugged myself tighter. The worn gown offered no shield or comfort.

Father Lammers spoke softly. "Kim, you are very special." He held out the crystal goblet in invitation.

I'd tasted the sacramental wine many times at Mass. I took the glass, lowered my eyes and whispered, "Thank you, Father." Its smell was different from the sacrificial wine. My eyes watered and stung as the pungent liquid brushed over my lips. I took a small sip and winced. I trembled and the wine sloshed around in the goblet, and threatened to spill.

Father Lammers liked to touch your privates on the playground, and it hurt.

I took a bigger gulp of the wine. It burned my throat and caused me to cough. I felt something was evil in this man of God and maybe even myself, but was not quite sure what.

You go to hell when you're bad.

I took another gulp of the wine.

When I looked up, he unzipped his pants.

My eyes widened and my heart raced, skipped, and felt explosive.

I didn't remember who led me back to my dorm. Clutching the Holy Card to my chest, I lay in bed and mouthed the words of my nightly prayer."Now I lay me down to sleep, I pray the Lord my soul to keep. If I should die before I wake, please give Father Lammers all my birthday cake." My words muddled up, slurred, "...cake day, birthday..."

I felt like I was sleeping awake. Moving standing still. I finally slept, not realizing that I was holding a lacy Holy Card of Saint Dymphna, the patron saint of molestation and rape victims.

Daybreak found me lagging behind, taking my time making my bed while the other girls rushed to be the first in line to attend to their morning hygiene. I looked at the sweet, smiling Saint painted so splendidly on the stiff card. I ran my fingers over the lacy frame as I scrutinized the face one last time.

A beautiful new Holy Card. Even worn or tattered, the Holy Cards became highly sought-after trophies, which we'd barter with another to obtain not-so-torn panties with a little elastic left, or a mismatched sock without the hole. I could never hold on to mine for long. Gayla would quickly take stock of my cards and finagle them away with ease.

I looked over at Jenny's iron bed and made a decision. I sneaked the prized Holy Card under my best friend's bedcovers to rid myself of its memory. And Jenny would marvel at its mysterious appearance and boast about her sudden unexplained fortune.

The morning breakfast brought no cheer, even though I sat with my sisters. After the Morning Prayer, I kept my head bowed and refused to answer their whispered questions. They stared at me with concern while whispering encouragements for me to eat. I toyed with the suspicious-looking gruel mix. A single slice of burnt dry toast lay untouched. Though not the usual oatmeal mix, it provided no consolation this morning.

Sister Deloris Marie struck my head to end my woolgathering. My sisters lowered their gazes and cowered expectantly. The nun delivered three additional strikes to each for good measure.

"You go to Father Lammers and clear his breakfast table this morning." She gave my head a thump with a metal spoon. "And don't bust up the china," she warned.

Pamela, Caity, and Gayla looked at me quizzically. Pamela leaned in and whispered, "Clearing Father Lammers's dining table is the big girls' duty." I could feel the color drain from my cheeks.

"Kimmi?" whispered Caity. She reached up and swept back the bangs on my forehead. "You're pale, you have dark circles."

I shrugged her off. "Leave me alone." I pouted.

Pamela reached for my hand but pulled away to avoid another strike from Sister Deloris Marie.

After breakfast, Sister Charlotte led our group back to the dorm. Regina taunted me by stepping on my heels, but I didn't rise to the bait. I was searching for something, and along the way I found it: a huge, eight-foot corkboard, hanging along the passage wall. Sister Katrina had just hung it last week. It exhibited the various art works done by the orphans.

I studied a drawing done in bright red chalks, creased my brow and moved in closer. Hesitantly, I looked over my shoulder then back to the board, and I reached my fingertips up to rub quick circles in the chalk. I brought my bright red fingertips down to my cheeks and blended in the chalky substance then quickened my step, catching up to the front of the line to align myself with Sister Charlotte. Stopping at the dorm's entryway, I waited to get the nun's attention.

Gathering all my courage, I accelerated my words. "Sister Charlotte, I'm ill with fever." I touched the back of my hand to my forehead, exaggerating the gesture. "I won't be able to clear Father Lammers's dining area. May I please be excused?" I waited. And as fate would have it, I delivered an ending to my pleas with a sloppy wet sneeze, compliments of the rising smell of chalk dust.

"I . . . I feel very sick . . .Very!" I wiped my nose with the back of my hand and linked them together quickly behind my back.

Sister Charlotte tilted my chin up and scrutinized me. My clown-circled chalk mask didn't conceal the dark shadows under my eyes.

"Straight to bed," she said.

I'd been holding my breath throughout Sister Charlotte's examination and now, making a quick escape to my bed, released a huge burst of air. Luckily for me, the old nun hadn't felt my forehead.

As I settled uneasily into my bed, Sister Charlotte came forward and administered a bitter-tasting liquid, which I accepted without complaint. Then I made a crucial, subconscious decision at this point: a decision which broke the nuns' rules requiring that all hands must be placed on top of your coverlet during sleep. I decided for some strange reason it would be safer if I started sleeping on my stomach with arms cradled close to my head. I learned later that this was a telltale sign of an abused child.

I dreamt of the witch again. She wore a long black robe, and this time a werewolf accompanied her. They chased me through mazes of dark narrow halls as thousands of leaves encircled me. Finally cornering me, the witch and werewolf grabbed me and shook me. Crying out, I awoke to find Sister Charlotte roughly shaking me.

I looked to the left of my bed and pointed to the stairwell door. "Sister Charlotte, the witch is back and she's living in the stairwell with a werewolf."

Sister Charlotte frowned, left the room, then returned with another large dose of the bitter-tasting liquid.

For two weeks I suffered the horrific nightmares. Within that time, my metal bed had been moved to three different areas of the dorm, but nothing would stop the nightmares. Soon my bed became the cold concrete floor outside Sister Charlotte's door. One morning she tripped right over me.

Finally, Sister Charlotte took me to Mother Superior. My feet dangled as I sat on the hard wooden bench outside Mother Superior's office and awaited my fate. I picked at the tiny balls of lint on my dress. My legs swung nervously back and forth. Back and forth. I wrung my hands and finally tucked them under my bottom to still them. After what seemed an eternity, the heavy wooden door opened. Sister Charlotte gestured for me to come forward. I could see my caregiver looked as weary as I felt.

I squirmed as I stood before Mother Superior, the tiny-framed nun who ran the orphanage. Looking down at the paperwork on her desk, she didn't so much as give me a glance. "It's been decided, Kim, and is now settled. You will move to Sister Anthony's dorm on the third floor."

Surprised, I looked at Sister Charlotte. That was my sister, Gayla's, dorm. A distant alarm rang in the back of my mind, but it was quickly replaced with joy at the prospect of being with Gayla.

Sister Charlotte and I walked in silence back to her dorm. She offered me a brown paper sack, and I smiled in anticipation of being with one of my sisters.

A ghostly smile crossed Sister Charlotte's mouth. I took a deep breath. And another. The witch wouldn't come to Sister Anthony's, not with the protection of my older sister there.

Carrying the small paper bag, which contained my life belongings, I quietly walked out of one ominous dorm and into another.

Ten
Where is Gayla?

I walked into Sister Anthony's quiet dorm and she grabbed a fistful of my hair, yelled, "Get into the bath line, your feet look like hoofs in a cow pie!"

Sister Anthony ran her dorm with stinging slaps and waspish words. Often the cruel, sadistic words inflicted upon us stung worse than the slaps. A red-headed nun, with small strawberry-puffs peeping out of her wimple, she had a fiery temper to match and stormy grey eyes. All of us would slink past her. It seemed I'd spent my whole life ducking and shrinking from the nuns' words and blows. The words and slaps were so frequent that, by reflex, I ducked low. It would seem abnormal to do otherwise.

Anyone so unlucky as to be in Sister Anthony's path was subject to her fury, without rhyme or reason.

I'd heard that Caity's earlier stay in her dorm had put her in Sister Anthony's way once too often. The misstep drew a slap that ruptured her eardrum. Soon after, Caity could not hear in her left ear.

Like Caity, Gayla became an easy target for Sister Anthony. She was about an inch taller than me, with a willowy body and a tomboyish face that was constantly streaked with dirt. With her dark brown hair, crudely chopped at ear level, and hazel eyes hidden behind glasses, she fell short of the nuns' standard for pleasant appearance. One morning, Sister Anthony grabbed Gayla by the hair and pulled her to her side, then caught my arm and yanked me forward. She jerked on Gayla's hair. "String-bean hair," she said. Then she grabbed my hair and pulled me to her side. "Gayla, why can't you wash your hair like your sister?" I yelped as the nun tugged harder on my hair. "See how Kim's hair shines?" she hissed.

Sister Anthony let go of my hair and gave us each a smack. "You couldn't possibly be sisters!" She smirked. "Gayla, you're filthy, no better than swine in a barn."

I fumed at the twisted compliments, offered the nun my silent dammits and Gayla's eyes welled up.

In the three weeks after moving from Sister Charlotte's dorm, my nightmares all but ceased, but my relief was overshadowed by my sister's sleepless nights. With each passing night, Gayla's dreams intensified, her cries awakening everyone in the dorm.

Gayla cried out, "Spiders," and I ran across the cold, dark floor to her. I shook her lightly and whispered, "Shush Gayla, Sister Anthony will—"

Sister Anthony snatched me away from the bed and pushed me down. She gave Gayla a hard slap and dragged us into the washroom. "Floors, tubs, and toilets," she barked. Two hours later we were done scrubbing and back in bed.

I overslept the next morning and scrambled out of bed, stumbling toward the washroom where I waited in line for an empty sink. A girl walked by and whispered in my ear, "Gayla's gone."

At early morning Mass, I searched the chapel.

"Gayla? Have you seen Gayla?" I asked all. "I can't find Gayla."

"Sister Anthony, I can't find Gayla," I said meekly, taking a step back. I wiped away a stray tear. She turned and walked away.

I received only stony glares that offered no clues.

I searched the halls as we headed toward breakfast, then I became desperate when I saw Caity and stepped out of the cafeteria line. Caity's dorm was passing, and I reached for her.

"Cat, I can't find Gayla."

She put her finger up to her mouth and shushed me, but Sister Deloris Marie appeared, caught the whisper and knocked Caity to the floor.

She rose slowly and I reached down to help her. Sister Deloris Marie yanked us both up by our hair and banged our heads together.

"Disobedient girls! Maybe an hour watching everyone else eat will teach you some respect."

She shoved us against the chipped concrete cafeteria wall. Hungry and aching, we watched the other orphans eat.

"I'm sorry for getting you in trouble, Cat." I gave a *dammit* to Sister Deloris Marie, no less than six times, until Caity cut me a warning.

"Kimmi, shush!"

"Dammit," I hissed one last time, then lowered my head.

After the cafeteria emptied, Sister Deloris Marie slapped a rag in our hands. "Floors, girls," she snarled.

We used our sudden misfortune to our advantage. While the smell of strong bleach watered our eyes and assailed our senses, our hands scrubbed. With hushed voices and guarded looks, we talked of Gayla's disappearance.

"Where do you think they're hiding her?" I asked.

"Maybe in the basement," Caity offered.

"Why, Cat? What if she's at City Hospital? What if she's dead?" I moaned. "The witch. Ohh. ..." I let out a small sob.

"Shush! Stop." She narrowed her eyes and went back to scrubbing.

"But, but—"

"We're in enough trouble. I said, stop it!" she warned.

As days and weeks passed without word from Gayla, I began to worry that the witch had come for my sister. My own nightmares returned, and I was eventually returned to Sister Charlotte's dorm.

I would not find any clues to Gayla's disappearance or to her whereabouts. I worried about the witch and Gayla. As the days passed my fears grew and generated stronger nightmares. Sister Charlotte's dorm offered no relief. It wasn't long until I reclaimed my old bed, the concrete spot outside the nun's private door.

Gayla returned a year later. With her reappearance came my second transfer to Sister Anthony's dorm, but no clue as to why Gayla had left or where she had been.

"Why don't you remember, Gayla?" I asked. "Was it the witch?" I grasped her shoulders.

"Go away." She shrugged then ran off, leaving me standing in confusion.

"Stop, Gayla! Come back here, Gayla," I hollered.

Later, throughout our adult lives, my other two sisters and I would wonder about the lost year of her life. How could one lose a whole year of their life? Isolation, hospitalization, locked somewhere away in a convent attic, we speculated.

Where did Gayla go? She never told us, and it would forever remain secret.

Eleven
Squandered innocence

I sat silent and swallowed back the secrets of my unshed tears. The movement of papers was the only sound. I smelled strong perfume and rubbed my temple to quash the impending headache I was sure to get from it.

I waited for the attorney's question, then looked at my hands resting on the table and tucked one quickly under my bottom. The never-ending gift from the nuns' over-corrections. My senses were on full alert, and I felt mistrust as the deposition dragged.

Why had I decided to become a coffee drinker today, of all days? Tea was my norm, and now I silently prayed to calm my caffeine jitters.

The nun leaned over and whispered to the attorney, then settled back into her seat and crossed her arms.

"Father Lammers's mole? Which hand was it on?" her attorney asked.

My heart hammered against my chest. I didn't want to remember. To force and provoke such memories seemed cruel and inhumane, especially since I'd hidden them so well. It all seemed surreal, as if I were telling the attorneys about someone else's nightmare.

Sitting across from the attorneys, I suddenly felt guilt not anger, I felt like the criminal not victim. And so was the intent, I realized.

My mother, Diane, had uncaringly brought four babies into the world. Subjecting us to violence and suffering, she had squandered the innocence of our childhood. Self-satisfaction and instant gratification were paramount throughout her own destructive, drug-filled life.

And Father Lammers? He who wore the face of God?

I studied the nun and her attorneys. I really need to work harder on my forgiveness issues. For months I'd been wrestling with the idea of dropping out of the lawsuit. I needed only one pretext, just one. Had it not been for my promise to support Caity, I wouldn't have hesitated.

Like a great pile of autumn leaves scattering into fall winds, my sisters and I had drifted apart after leaving Saint Thomas - Saint Vincent Orphan Asylum. We would go for years sometimes without hearing from each other. All of us were too busy trying to overcome our childhood traumas, and each of us plunged forward alone. That was hard enough.

My sweet sister Caity was fighting her own battle with cancer while the self-destructive problem child, Gayla, had become her mother's daughter. Gayla, lost to alcohol and drugs, forever fighting demons, which would eventually win.

And my eldest sister, Pamela, had become another statistic. Dead in her twenties, she lost her battle to the demons of her past. I'd still never come to terms with this, for it was fate that took Pamela, and even crueler that Pamela's passing had happened on my birthday. A constant yearly reminder, it saddened all my birthday celebrations.

And would God punish me?

How in the world could I punish others? The physical demons of my youth no longer existed. Dead. All dead!

Somebody take this wheel before I crash, my mind screamed. I shifted in my chair and fought the fear. I zoned out all the other currents, my sisters, my mother, slowed my breathing, and willed calm.

For a moment, I thought about the brides of Christ, and it occurred to me that they had been manipulated and controlled by the Catholic Church. I'd read and understood that spanning centuries and up to the 1970s at least, many women and children were forced into convents for various reasons, mostly due to poverty: mouths simply couldn't be fed, nor minds educated. Widows were stripped of their lands and possessions by this religion. For many, their marriage to Christ had been debased in the foulest way, raped by cloaked clergy. And for one brief moment I felt compassion for their lost innocence, and I realized the dysfunction of these innocents – my nuns among them.

The magnitude of abuses was vast, subterranean and far beyond the healthy mind's comprehension. Again, secrets and mysteries and oh so many victims. Too many. My attorney, William, had already given voice to so many victims before me. But the voice of those previous victims, abused by the Catholic Church, grew somewhat louder with the presence of support from their former family units. They hadn't been orphans.

I studied the nun and I thought, was it *fair* to punish?

I wavered between guilt and rage. If I could only grab my anger and keep it. Instead, a heavy burden of sadness cloaked me, weighed me down, causing confusion.

It would be so easy to forgive and be done. But no, I needed to stand strong. Oh, I don't know what I need anymore.

"Left. I believe the mole was on his left."

I settled deeper into my seat, looked at the opposing attorneys, then retreated into a defense mode, crossing my arms.

"Have you spoken to anyone about the abuses of your childhood? Anyone? Counselors?"

"I told you, I have told no one about the abuses. Well, with the exception of Mrs. Lindauer, the state social worker of my youth, long gone now."

What would Mrs. Lindauer say? I wondered. She had been Catholic. I brought my knuckle up to my mouth to stifle a sob.

Mrs. Lindauer would say, "Be brave, Kim." I touched my bracelet. I believed in my heart she knew the origin and meaning behind the beaded bracelet when she had gifted it to me long ago.

I had certainly not known at the time that the scarab beads were an amulet, a strong symbol of protection. To Kimmi, the orphan, the bracelet held only the whispered promises of hope.

I gritted my teeth and realized I no longer gave a damn about the Catholic Church, that my give-a-damns for the Church had long been broken, shattered into infinite shards, and that realization was both powerful and terrifying.

I felt as if I were abandoning God, my soul. I prayed for forgiveness. I wished I could talk to God about it, to myself, but my voice screamed silence. And I would hold on to that silence as long as I could. After all, I knew one couldn't expect to walk away from the battlefield victorious without carrying wounds and lasting scars. Silence would be one of those scars.

And with age came more silence, sprinkled with wisdom and knowledge. But, if I didn't come to terms with this and face my past soon, it would become a future hazard.

And lest I forget, there were Pamela, Caity, and Gayla. And so many others. The list was depressingly endless.

I rubbed my temple. The perfume had done the trick. I needed another Tylenol for my rebounding headache, rebounding childhood. I smoothed the fabric of my green jacket.

I asked the attorney to repeat her question.

Twelve
The dance

Sister Anthony released the collar of the oversized dress that swallowed my seven-year-old body. I stumbled back and reached up to rub the neck-burn she'd left.

"Do I have to repeat the question again?" Sister Anthony spat. "Where did you get that red dress?"

"My sister —"

"Take it off and get rid of it, and get in line for bath."

It was six-fifteen, bath time. The ever-quiet dorms of Saint Thomas came alive with the rattles and rumbling of water vibrating throughout the building's old iron pipes. The jaunty roar of fluid song and whispered voice was my favorite, as it punctuated the nights with the approaching promise of escape through slumber.

Everyone was lining up for our evening ritual of brushing teeth, taking baths, and preparing for bed.

"Yes, Sister Anthony." I got in the line forming outside the washroom.

I peeked around the corner and saw the small enameled sinks were occupied. I looked to the left and saw girls moving quickly around the corner of the long, thin wall that hid the twenty-two narrow lockers that held our meager borrowed belongings.

Squeaks, clanging of metal, and running water rose above whispers. Straight ahead were two tubs and two toilets. Occupied. I waited for one of the wooden swinging half-doors to open. Growing impatient, I pushed past Regina and went to my locker.

After retrieving my gown, I brushed my teeth, then waited beside Byrdie for an empty tub room.

"We're next, Byrdie." I smiled.

I watched as Sister Anthony slipped out of the washroom for her evening prayers and saw the two nuns from the boys' side slip in. Sister Mary Francis and Sister Mon-Marie watched over us like hawks. They leaned casually against the tiny sinks. We moved quietly and quickly, avoiding the nuns at all costs.

Any nun from the boys' side instilled fear. They were usually taller and bigger, and these Sisters were too.

The small tub room emptied and Byrdie and I walked in. I sat down and leaned against the half-ceramic tiled wall that concealed the tub and waited for Byrdie to finish her bath.

For as long as I could remember, Byrdie Maize had been at Saint Thomas. It seemed only natural that she was here, but to the nuns it was anything but. Byrdie was African-American and the only child of color at Saint Thomas. At least, the only one I knew about. Referred to as Black Byrdie by the nuns, she ducked lower and slunk more cautiously than any of us. Her only crime was her color. The nuns' perpetual fury was fueled by the mere presence of Byrdie, who too often incurred wrath born of bigotry.

When Byrdie first came to Saint Thomas, her hair had been shaved within an eighth of an inch of her head, and that was how it remained. The nuns insisted they wouldn't "touch that nappy head," and kept it shaved off, not only to prevent lice, but also so the nuns wouldn't have to wash it until Byrdie grew old enough to wash it herself.

Byrdie was tall and slightly plump. Her skin was dark and smooth and her expressive black eyes always sparkled. Her dimpled face was always wide with a grin. But her color couldn't mask the bruises and cuts, which were always present.

She was gifted with an unusually lovely singing voice, like the slow dripping of liquid cinnamon. It was soothing, lilting.

Byrdie's mother had died, and her daddy had abandoned her to the orphanage. The brutal tortures she suffered at Saint Thomas far outweighed those of any of the other orphans. We children tried to shield Byrdie as best we could against her monsters, for we all loved her dearly.

Still, Byrdie kept her sweetness and would profess to all that her daddy would be coming soon and would be taking her to California. At night, and in whispered unison, we prayed, "O Almighty God, please have Byrdie's daddy come and get her real soon. We beseech thee, Amen."

I would hug her on the final day of my own departure from Saint Thomas. Byrdie would smile sweetly and say, "Kimmi, did I tell you, my daddy's coming this weekend to take me away to California?"

"Six-thirty," the two nuns cuckooed.

I sat up straight, peeked around the ceramic wall and interrupted Byrdie's singing. "Hurry Byrdie," I warned, "it's six-thirty. Only fifteen minutes 'til inspection." She continued singing. "Byrdie?"

Without warning, black robes rushed past me, knocking me to the floor. The sound of the wooden door cracking against ceramic wall interrupted the beautiful voice within.

Byrdie was dragged from the tub by the two nuns.

"Byrdie!" I reached up to Byrdie and Sister Mary Francis kicked me in my side with her heavy-toed shoe. I winced, sucked in a breath, jumped up and followed the threesome.

Water splashed and dripped everywhere. Byrdie's eyes were wide and startled, and she was placed naked in the middle of the washroom. Sister Mary Francis pulled her by the ear to center her in front of our bewildered stares.

The nun cackled, "You ain't nevah gonna wash that nasty black off your body, and since you can waste so much time

singing, Byrdie Maize, why don't ya jus dance a little jig for us."
She yanked hard on Byrdie's ear again. "Dance!"

Dripping wet, cold and naked, Byrdie was forced to dance
until the nuns tired of it.

"Dance, Byrdie," the two nuns jeered and clapped liked two
angry penguins. "Dance a jig!"

Much to my horror and embarrassment, I was forced to
watch in silence with the rest of the girls. My face burned with
hatred for the nuns. For the first time ever, I experienced this new
emotion that trembled my entire being. It threatened to spew out
like steam from a hissing pressure-cooker. It was a powerful
sensation that alarmed me, and for a moment I felt faint.

After tiring of their obscene amusement, the nuns took
Byrdie into the bathroom. They dunked her head into the toilet
water, then brought her to stand before us.

We stood silent, tears flowing.

Sister Mary Francis slapped Byrdie upside the head with a
wire scrub brush, slammed her to the floor and ordered her to
scrub the entire washroom area, naked. Then she pointed her fat,
stubby finger at us, and boomed, "Bed."

The dorm was restless that night and sleep didn't come easy
for us. Sobs and sniffles filled the dorm's darkness. I tossed and
turned most of that night. I tried covering my head, burying it
with my tear-stained pillow to drown out Byrdie's whimpers,
which floated across the room. Hours later, Byrdie's crying melted
into low, soulful song, which eventually lulled me into restless
slumber.

A few days later, Byrdie disappeared for a few weeks.

The overheard conspiratorial whispers of the nuns would
reveal that she'd suffered pneumonia and was taken to City
Hospital.

Thirteen
The nurturer

Gayla leaned over to me, pointed and whispered, "There's Pamela and Caity's dorm."

My sisters passed by, each taking a feathered grip of my hand. I smiled big.

I was struggling to survive from each day to the next unaware that Caity and Pamela were fighting their own battles. But the whispers and my knowledge grew as I grew. I understood little at age five, barely more at age six. But when I was seven, I understood more of the words I heard and the incidents I saw.

With her rare beauty, Pamela had quickly become the nuns' *darling* child.

Her hair was a dark chestnut and hung longer. It was a striking contrast to my short dark- blonde hair. Pamela's face held a classic beauty with china blue eyes and the skin of a finely crafted porcelain doll. Good-natured, non-defiant, quiet and reserved, she was able to escape some of the abuses that we suffered but certainly not all.

There was a small handful of other orphans who fell into this category as well. For whatever reasons, they all resembled each other in character and startling good looks.

Caity was not so lucky, and even though Pamela was the eldest, Caity was considered the nurturing earth mother. A constant worrier at too early an age, she'd always been the protector, provider, and comforter. She fussed over us and would follow this pattern throughout young adulthood as well.

Caity's small build was enveloped by a corduroy dress, and her light brown hair fell in soft curls. Sadly, her sweet face was obscured by a pair of cat-eyed glasses held together with dirty band-aids, which made her an easy target.

Survival at Saint Thomas meant blending in, avoiding the attention of the nuns who were all too eager to find an outlet for their cruel whims.

Caity's other major sins seemed to be that she was left-handed and a sleepwalker, which would become a major detriment for her. Her small hands were always swollen and red from repeated whacks -- utensils, rulers, or whatever happened to be handy to the nuns, especially the ones who taught her class and presided over the cafeteria. They insisted that Caity use only her right hand. The nuns had broken both her pinky fingers and a middle finger with their vicious over-corrections. It reminded me of when I'd earned my broken pinky finger from a nun during my early instruction in penmanship.

But Caity's sleepwalking caused her to suffer the most. Wandering eerily around the dorms at night, Caity spent her sleeping time arranging the other orphans' bed covers. By tucking them in and fussing with their covers, she appeared to be a dwarfed little mother to all.

It was somewhat amusing as well as endearing, but not necessarily so when one was the unexpected recipient of such mothering. This especially held true because of Caity's poor eyesight and sleep state combined to make her pull the bed-covers over your head and tuck them neatly under your thin-ticked mattress – unexpected, almost laugh inducing.

When Caity graduated to Sister Martin's dorm at age nine, the nun was unaware of Caity's sleepwalking, but she learned soon enough and waged war against her. Her weapon of choice was a two-foot black razor strap, which she used relentlessly and often.

Caity suffered the beatings for well over a year until an unexpected visit from a State social worker. The beatings stopped only to be replaced by a new terror. Sister Martin decided she would stop the sleepwalking by tying Caity up at bedtime.

Through all this, I didn't have the heart to burden my sisters with my *Oatmeal Tears*. But to my dismay I consumed a lot more of my oatmeal-vomit mixed breakfast during Caity's tortured times. Even if I asked, Caity could not be reached, for she was lost in her own oppressed world.

Someone stole my sister's tears, and I couldn't share. I was slowly losing my own.

Mass ran over one morning and I was delighted to be sitting with my sisters for breakfast. I glanced over at my bigger sister, but Caity now kept her head lowered to her dinnerware.

"Caity," I pleaded. With my thumb and forefinger, I reached up and tried to pry open her eye. "What's wrong? Cat?"

"Stop it," she snapped. "Stop it now; you're always getting us into trouble!"

My eyes welled up. "Cat," I whimpered.

Caity glared at me and I shrank back against the chair. Sister Deloris Marie took notice and fisted her palm, knocking Caity to the floor. I wailed in anguish, for my sister's suffering and my own broken heart.

Caity's suffering continued without interruption. Her sleepwalking had become a waking nightmare. For a year and a half, Caity's feet and hands were tightly bound every night, secured to her metal bed by thick ropes, which restricted all movement.

Sister Martin took twisted pleasure in Caity's weaknesses, and the demon showed no heart. If Caity needed to go to the bathroom, she'd have to do so in bed. The razor strap was brought out on these occasions when she couldn't control her bodily fluids.

Learning quickly, she would painfully hold her bladder till dawn's arrival and the release of the ropes. She'd walk turtle-like to the bathroom, bent over like an old lady. Bladder and kidney infections followed and remained throughout adulthood.

Sister Martin never broke Caity's sleepwalking, but whether or not she broke Caity's spirit was debatable. But it wasn't long till Caity gained an ally, a new friend: Sister Joseph Michael.

Sister Joseph Michael delighted in Caity's presence. She became attached to her, and the other girls would tease Caity and accuse her of being a pet. Caity and Sister Joseph Michael were inseparable; one only had to look for one to find the other.

Even my sisters and I were jealous of Caity's close friendship with Sister Joseph Michael. And I did not like the nun.

Once, Caity had grabbed me on the playground, and asked me to accompany her to the basement to meet Sister Joseph Michael. I hung behind my sister as Sister Joseph Michael welcomed Caity with a huge hug and kiss. Caity reached for my hand, pulling me in front of her, and Sister Joseph Michael seemed surprised to see me. She was scary and had manly looks. I was not happy, and jealousy reared its ugly head. So I whined and complained to my other sisters. When they questioned Caity about Sister Joseph Michael, she would go beet red, stammer, and wave her hand dismissively into the air.

Father Lammers finally gave the dismissal for Mass to end, but not before he'd let it run over a good twenty minutes. Grateful for mixed blessings, I hurried into the cafeteria knowing a late Mass would mean sitting with my sisters.

Smiling, I took my seat next to Caity, joined in the Morning Prayer, then picked up the dry toast in front of me and waved it in front of her. "Cat? I have something to tell you." I stuffed a wad of toast into my mouth. Pamela raised her brow, gave warning, and I hurriedly choked down my bread before speaking again.

I glanced over my shoulder and whispered, "Cat, we watched *Lost In Space* on the new television again last night."

Caity perked up. "We got to see it last week."

The orphanage had received its first television set not long before, and on rare occasions, and as reward for good behavior, the nuns would let us watch it. *Lost In Space* was the choice and it soon became my favorite, almost surpassing my beloved, old-reeled, Shirley Temple classics. I would always imagine and hope, I'd be swept away from Saint Thomas, sucked into outer space with the characters from *Lost In Space*, Penny and Will Robison, and the Robot—my trusted allies.

"Cat, I overheard the big girls talking, and Bonnie said they might run away. Maybe we can run away to space and live like Penny and—"

"I hear Robot warning Danger, Kimmi. Danger." Gayla grunted in Robot-speak, then went back to eating her breakfast.

I frowned. "Cat, maybe we should try."

Caity picked at her toast, finally set it aside, then pushed herself away from the table. "Meet me outside the back stairwell at six-fifteen tonight." She stood.

"But that's bath time and it'll be dark. If we get caught we'll—"

"Shhh," she bent over, "six-fifteen."

I slipped out of the bath line at six-ten, made my way through the dorm's sleeping quarters and tiptoed down the back stairwell. Grabbing the metal knob, I quietly exited to the outside.

I stomped my feet a couple of times to still the knock of my knees quaking my body and waited. I stared out into the darkness, then released a heavy sigh when I saw a small dark figure approach from the big girls' wing. Caity grabbed my hand.

"What took you so long? I've been waiting *forever*." I glanced over my shoulder. "If Sister finds out I'm gone—"

She raised her finger to her mouth. "Shhh, we have to be quiet."

"What do we need to do to run? Bonnie says they'll run away soon."

"Kimmi, just focus on the stars. Pray, pray hard and if you pray hard enough . . ."

I looked up at Caity. "Then, we'll go into *Lost In Space* like Will and Penny? You promise, okay?"

She nodded and grabbed my hand and squeezed tight.

I closed my eyes and started praying, then after a minute, gave into temptation. Opening an eye, I peeked upward and caught the twinkle of stars and decided to blend and add some strong wish-upon-a-star wishes to my prayer for good measure.

After a few more minutes, I looked up at Caity. Her eyes were closed, scrunched tight behind her band-aid-rim glasses.

I tugged on her sleeve. "I want to run away like Bonnie says." I looked up at the night sky, doubtful, then peered out at the road leading out of the orphanage. I pointed. "Out there."

Caity studied the road, then clamped my hand and started pulling me toward the road.

"No! Wait." I jerked my hand out of hers, smoothed the sides of my dress and shook my head. She reached for me and I moved away. "I have to get back upstairs and take my bath before Sister Anthony finds out I'm gone. I . . . I want to, but, but I . . ." My voice jumped then fell like a parachuted whisper. "I'm too afraid."

I looked at the tall brick walls of the orphanage, wiped away a tear and turned toward the stairwell door. I reached for the metal knob. "Too afraid."

Caity's voice was faint, no stronger than a star's final wink in the cosmos. "I'm too afraid not to."

I don't recall seeing any more new bruises on Caity, but I do remember it wasn't long after our *Lost In Space* misadventure that I noticed Caity's *Good Ship Lollipop* had gone quietly out to sea: lost. She had become distant, withdrawn and evasive.

Many years later as adults, we sisters talked, and I learned Sister Joseph Michael had been hugging Caity with her hands, not her heart.

The caring nurturer, Sister Joseph Michael, had turned out to be a monster: a molester.

Fourteen
Beauty, being in the eye of the beholder

"I'm painting a monster." Regina boasted.

I rolled my eyes, dismissed her and directed my attention back to Sister Katrina's conversation. The young nun was new to Saint Thomas and had quickly become the orphans' favorite. Sister Katrina was somewhat of an ally and championed successfully for the art board, as well as a few stingy pieces of broken chalk for the playground.

"Yes, Sister, if you could spare the time, I'll supply the paper," Sister Katrina said. She folded her hands and waited.

"An art exhibit? Wasted time," muttered Sister Daniel. "I don't know if I can allow the interruption."

Most of the daily school time was marred by constant interruption, wasted time. Rulers whooshed madly through the air, aimed at the knuckles of unsuspecting students. The sting of thoughtless, cruel criticism would hit its mark, reducing us to tears.

I watched and listened as the nuns' conversation continued. Sister Daniel's face was getting red. Sister Katrina smiled when Sister Daniel raised her hands in defeat and turned away.

"There will be an art exhibit." Sister Daniel went on to explain, in a sour tone, "One winner will be selected to receive a small prize for their work."

With quiet attention we listened while she slapped a piece of blank construction paper upon each desk.

"Sheer waste and stupidity!" she stated.

I sat in class and twirled a strand of hair.

For well over a week, I'd done little but stare at the paper, my mind as blank as the page in front of me. I loved art and had become modestly good for a child of seven. A few of the visiting nuns had actually praised my previous works.

I sat and looked at my blank page. The contest deadline was fast approaching: only two days left. With each passing day came more slaps and more harsh words from Sister Daniel, who insisted I start and complete my project without further interruption. Sister Daniel's actions only increased my apprehension.

After much agonizing thought I finally decided on a collage of brightly colored flowers. Satisfied with the idea, I'd cover my entire paper with them. With my tongue hanging out to one side and my mouth contorting with each stroke of my artist's brush, I immersed myself in my work.

Throughout the project, Sister Daniel would pass by and randomly grab an artwork off a student's desk. She'd wave it carelessly through the air. "Chicken scratch, a waste of paper and time."

The swishing of long black robes alerted me and, cringing with fear, I covered my art with my arm. As I paused to contemplate where to place my last two flowers, I received a startling slap from Sister Daniel. "You've wasted enough time. Quit dawdling and get back to work."

The unexpected interruption caused me to knock the artwork onto the floor. As I bent over to retrieve it, Sister Daniel stepped purposely on it. I rose quickly, in retreat. My elbow knocked the tiny jar of dark rinse water onto the top of Sister Daniel's shoe and spilled onto my artwork.

Horrified that my beautiful artwork was damaged, I looked tearfully up to the nun. She gave me a tight, smug smile and ground her foot into my paper. I heard a rip. Then she picked up my artwork, waved the soaked, paint-smeared paper madly about the room as she hollered at me. "Your chicken-scratch work will be exhibited as is. This will teach you not to waste valuable time and apply yourself harder in the future."

"Sister Daniel, please. One more chance, one more piece of paper?"
She turned away with a nasty smirk.

Much to my dismay, two days later I found my offensive artwork centered on the art board.

For the next two weeks I suffered the embarrassment and humiliation of my exhibit. I would hurry to reach the board and try to block a passing dorm's view of my work by standing in front of it.

Toward the end of the art exhibit, Sister Katrina approached me as I stood in front of the board. She studied the ruined artwork. After a while she told me that the work was unique and would be considered Abstract. "In the water-stained streaks, one can almost see other shapes beginning to take form in the picture. Don't you see it as well?" she asked.

Patiently she explained that beauty was in the eye of the beholder.

I tried to sound out Sister Katrina's phrase. I didn't understand it, but I thought the words were pretty.

The next morning as I walked to the cafeteria, I stepped up my pace as I approached the art board. Preparing myself to stand and block my work, I stepped back instead, amazed. Pinned onto the corner of my art was a big blue ribbon. Beside it was a handwritten note card stating, Best Abstract Art.

Tugging on Regina's arm, I pulled her to the board and proudly showed her the art and ribbon.

"That's plain ol' ugly!" insisted Regina. Her freckles danced on her face. "Dirt ugly!" she spat. She swung her leg back. I laughed and jumped to the side, easily missing the kick. Regina scowled and threatened another, but I promptly stepped forward, pinched her arm, and flicked the air over her right shoulder.

"Ouch, you devil! It's ugly—spit dirt ugly." Regina screeched.

"Why Regina Croft! You just better flick that nasty ol' devil off your shoulder! Tut, tut, tut. And no, it's not ugly, it's abstracturated! ABSTRACTURATED, and you just don't have any beauty beholder in your eye!" Proudly, I stepped aside to show my prize to all who passed the art board.

The next day found me bursting with pride as Sister Katrina called out my name. I jumped out of my desk and hurried over to her. Pinning the blue ribbon on my dress at the front of the class, I grinned widely while Sister Daniel stood to the side and fumed.

When Sister Katrina left the schoolroom, Sister Daniel tossed all the artwork, including mine, in the metal waste can beside her desk.

"Now we can finally do something constructive! Get out your math assignment," she demanded.

Sister's math book crashed down and sawed through the chalk-dust quiet. In unison, we all jumped.

Fifteen
Foolish sage

2005

A cell phone rang, and I jumped. The lengthy deposition was draining me. My mind had wandered. Then the hourglass clogged.

I looked at the surrounding attorneys to check for any signs of physical or emotional wear. The opposing attorneys looked no worse for wear. They'd been conditioned to withstand the humdrum of long legal depositions.

Sighing, I reminded myself to proceed with caution. Too many questions whiplashed around my family, my children. Fear squeezed my heart.

I knew the Church was clever and cunning in retrieving information, but I had let my guard down, and I'd just found out the information that proved it.

I thought back to the revealing day that had confirmed these suspicions, and once again I broke out in a cold sweat. I had been out running errands when I'd answered my cell phone. The caller, another parent from my child's school, had talked hurriedly and in hushed tones. It seems she had been in the school's office just moments before, when the archdiocese of Louisville came digging around for information regarding my family.

I pulled my car over and felt the blood drain from my face. One stipulation on joining the lawsuit was being able to use my maiden name. And for the privacy and protection of my family, I'd signed my name to the lawsuit as such.

Long ago, Joe and I had made the decision to seek the finest level of education for our children that we could afford. I had fears and doubts about returning to the Church, but in the end I reluctantly agreed to admit our last school-aged child into the Catholic school system. Our son had attended a Christian school, but he had graduated long ago and moved out into the world. I'd really wanted my children to have the best educational advantages, the freedoms of academic teachings coupled with a Christian environment, and at the time it seemed to be in the Catholic school system.

We'd chosen a small parish, and I'd painstakingly built a ten-year relationship with some of its members. Over a decade to build and one measly minute to tear it all down. How would I find the strength to face these parish members again? I had become close to many good and kind parishioners, and many of their children played with mine. Some might view it as betrayal, while others, I knew, would feed off the circumstances, adding gossip to misfortunes.

I swallowed hard. They had found my child. I'd been foolish. The cell phone suddenly felt venomous. I heard the calling parent's words but wasn't listening anymore.

Cold terror struck quick, piercing my heart. I felt words colliding, and suddenly it became hard to focus. I squinted my eyes and rubbed my forehead. The parent calling had smugly delivered the news and was now looking for gossip, waiting for a reaction. I dismissed her in mid-sentence with a click of the cell's End button. Then I threw the phone to the passenger's side.

My mind raced as I tried to digest the unwelcome news. Shaking and furious, I reached for my cell phone and punched in three wrong numbers before reaching William McMurry's office.

"He's not in," the secretary said. "May I ask—?"

I shook my head. My wrath couldn't wait. "This is Kim. Find him. I don't care where he is, where he's sitting. Just find him!" I threw the phone on the seat again.

Driving my car back into traffic, I changed direction and headed home. I felt numb, dazed, and the ring of my cell phone rattled my thoughts.

"Kim? It's William."

"My child! They found out. Who gave out this information?" I snapped.

"What the...?"

"They found my child, my daughter! They showed up at her school!" I raged. "Did you give it out?"

"No, I did not! Kim, listen—"

"My daughter! I thought they wouldn't find me. By signing my maiden name, I thought I'd be protected. How—"

"No. We went over this, Kim, in our initial interview. I told you then, yes, you could use your maiden name, but Kentucky law does not allow a suit to be filed anonymously like many other states."

"But—"

"You need to get counseling, to tell her about your childhood. You—"

There was an edge to his voice I hadn't heard before.

"No! She's a teen." I gritted my teeth. "And in a Catholic high school. They'll use it against her!" I clenched my fist. "She's got her plate full without carrying around my screwed-up childhood baggage."

"Listen, I've seen this before with others. Counseling would—"

"No!" My eyes filled with tears, and the phone shook in my hand. My words stagnated, threatened to suffocate me. I lowered the phone to my lap and stared into nowhere, fighting for control. Taking a deep breath, and in angry denial, I slowly shook my head, then raised the phone back to my ear. "Stop!" I demanded. "They're getting too close to my family."

Too late, I thought. I released a whistle between clenched teeth. I flinched. *What the?* Damn if I didn't feel as if I'd just been profiled. His counseling suggestion amplified my anger. I didn't need William's expertise or pacifying advice on how to manage my emotions. He would offer up counseling as habit, sage knowledge, as his education directed him to do.

So this was how he dealt with raw emotions, with others' and mine?

"Well, I'm not the others!" I'm Kim. *Strong.* Why can't you see me as a person, not a cluster! "Counseling?" I fumed. "Hah! As though a psych counselor *could* slay my closet monsters, protect my family and make nice with the past. I don't need to get my head screwed on straight, I need justice. And that's *your* job, William McMurry!" Angry tears rained down to puddle in my mind.

He made me cry? How could that be? He was nothing more than a stranger. Really, nothing more, and I'd do well to remember such. He would always be a stranger. "Screw justice, screw you, William McMurry, and save your damn sagacious recommendations for those who need them." *Just screw it all,* I thought.

I held the phone away from my face. Branding-iron hot, sizzling plastic vaporized all reason; our phones exploded with challenge, matching the heat of our tempers.

"Then maybe you should just drop out of the suit. I'll mail you the release," he snapped.

"Fine! That's fine with me, William!" I fired back, then clicked the End button.

Looking around, I found myself sitting in my driveway. Disoriented, I couldn't believe I'd driven all the way home during our heated conversation. Fury subsided as reality set in. No wonder there were so many cell phone-related car accidents.

Stunned by my actions, I didn't even remember the route I had just taken. I took a deep breath, slowly diffusing my emotions as I lowered my head to the steering wheel. Blinking hard, I reached my hand up and wiped away the stinging tears on my cheeks. It wouldn't do for my family to see me like this.

Weakening, I delivered a punch to the dash. "Bastards." Just the thought of those bastards so close to my child made me sick with fear.

Conciliatory thoughts slowly took hold and made me regret my words to William. After all, he hadn't promised protection or anonymity. He couldn't stop the Church from digging around. And he was on my side. Still, pride kept me from calling him back to apologize. This was his hiccup, my chance to bail.

William called back in a few weeks, a little after nine o'clock on a Sunday morning. Searching, but I didn't know for what. I didn't give him a chance. He offered his cell number, and I rudely refused it, saying I'd catch him at the office if I needed him.

I blew him off like an unexpected raw northern wind, and I felt awful afterwards, going so far as to mentally stomp my foot to shake my foolish, stubborn pride.

Dammit, Kim, look into your rearview and kick your pride to the curb. But William could have at least given a heads-up.

Joe startled me by walking into the room just as I was hanging up. "Who was that?"

I walked over to him, gave him a quick kiss and brushed past him.

"Hon, who —?" he began.

"Uhmm, just a stranger," I called over my shoulder. "A stranger. Really, no one," I whispered.

I called Caity later and told her I couldn't handle the intrusive lawsuit. I was sorry, but wished to bail. Caity readily agreed with me, saying she wished to withdraw from the lawsuit as well.

"Huh?"

"Too stressful and I need to concentrate on my illness," Caity said.

This blew me away, and I turned the conversation around. "Caity, stay strong, stay focused on your path." To insure that she would do so, I reluctantly pledged my support back to her and into the lawsuit. "I'm with you, Cat."

Disgusted by the archdiocese's earlier prying, I now directed my eyes toward the deposing attorneys in renewed distrust.

Sixteen
Black-eyed peas

2005

I'd been denying the emotional wear of the lawsuit by trying to fight sleep to the point I no longer trusted or welcomed sweet slumber. I bolted straight up. I'd been falling toward earth and finally hit ground. It felt like I had just died and been slammed back to life, an eerie, calming sensation. My face was wet with tears as I peered over to see my husband sleeping peacefully. I finally swallowed my fear and shrugged it off. It wasn't the first time. These night tremors started after the beginning of the lawsuit and were becoming more frequent.

My stomach rolled and I barely made it to the bathroom. My body felt cold and weak. I climbed back into bed and made a mental note to call my doctor. I groaned as I looked over to my alarm clock—it was past nine o'clock. The phone rang and I fumbled, dropped the receiver and headed toward the kitchen so I wouldn't awaken Joe.

"Kim, you hermit!" Mikea said over the phone. "I haven't seen you in months. Sam and I expect you and Joe tomorrow night at seven sharp. Roast and black-eyed peas!"

"I … all right, all right. Sounds great, Mik."

Mikea was one of my childhood friends. We'd gone to school together. After I'd left the orphanage at age ten, I was passed off to several relatives and ended up living with my maternal grandmother in one of those small, dust bowl, bible-thumping towns. Mikea was a free-spirited army brat and, what with my frequent relocations, we'd quickly become close friends. But I never told Mikea I'd grown up in an orphanage until we were well into our twenties. I was too afraid she'd use it against me during our teenage years during some imbalanced hormonally-charged teenage catfight, which we had from time to time.

When we arrived, Mikea smiled, grabbed my arm and pulled me inside. Joe headed toward Sam's garage to tool around with an old pickup. I sat on her couch with her cat resting comfortably on my lap. I scratched his ears and looked up at Mikea. Usually we happily tripped all over one another's words. But tonight there was an uncomfortable silence.

Mikea finally looked at me with her big blue peeps, swept back her long, chestnut strands, and said casually, "Kim, my uncle died a couple of weeks ago."

"I'm sorry, Mik. I didn't know. I've been so busy. Teddy, right?"

"Yeah. Teddy. He was seventy-five." She raised a brow, then added, "Busy hiding."

I winced at Mikea's insight. Silence. Then out of the blue Mikea said, "Teddy raped me when I was six."

"What? Ohh, Mik—"

"Know what, Kim?" she went on, "I told my mom after the funeral. I told her I'd been raped when I was six. Mom asked, 'Who?' Before I could answer her, Mom added, 'Oh I bet I know, it was my dad, your grandpa. Right?' "

My jaw dropped. I'd known Mikea forever, thought I knew everything about her. Her mother's response also told me that her mother had been raped by her own father. That just blew me away. I shook my head and gave her a hug. "I'm so sorry."

Mikea just looked at me and smiled. Then she started singing "Goodbye Earl," the Dixie Chicks' song about poisoned black-eyed peas being fed to Earl, an abusive husband, by his wife and her best friends, to retaliate for the abuse. The meal resulted in Earl's demise.

I laughed and joined in. We finally stopped and I jokingly said, "Hey, Mik, you know all those dinners we burnt when we first started cooking? We should've invited Teddy and done a 'Goodbye Earl' on him, with one of your black-eyed pea dinners."

For some reason Mikea thought that was hysterical. She rolled off the couch and onto the floor, kicked up her legs and laughed until tears fell. For a few moments I laughed with her. I was happy that her tears came from release, the release one gets from burying one's monsters. Then I paused, creased my brow and thought of William. Mikea knew nothing about my past abuses or the impending lawsuit.

Mikea kept laughing, her tears now streaming down her face. I was starting to get uneasy. I wanted her to stop, but she started singing "Goodbye Earl" again. I shook my head, grimaced and looked at my friend lying on the floor singing. I was getting nervous.

I waited for her to stop. I worried that she was going to have one of those over-the-edge meltdowns, the dark ones, the ones you never return from. I yelled, "Hey Mik, stop! Mikea, you okay? Chill!"

She stopped singing and stared at me. For a minute, green eyes merged with blue, turned oceanic and I could see her fear. She was scared, and she knew she'd scared me. Jumping up, she headed toward the kitchen and called over her shoulder, "You must be starved. You're getting too small, Kim." Then she stopped, turned and said, "Hey you, Miss Always So Cool, Miss Always In Control, anytime you want to share, I'm here. C'mon, call the guys in. Help me set the table."

I flinched, looked down at the jeans I was wearing and realized I wasn't wearing my size four jeans. I was wearing my teen's size one jeans, which I'd grabbed by mistake. And I'd been sitting very comfortably in them. An uncomfortable thought crossed my mind.

I don't feel well.

The next day, I made an appointment with my doctor. The receptionist was kind enough to pencil me in the same day for a two o'clock.

"Okay, so what's up with you?" the doctor asked. He flipped the pages on my medical chart. "You had a physical not long ago. Numbers are better than most eighteen-year-olds'," he added.

He reached for his stethoscope.

I took a couple of deep breaths, and waited for him to finish listening to my heart and lungs. Then he sat down on the stool in front of me. "Okay," he said."You look great, trim as usual."

I shifted uncomfortably, sat on my hands and looked past him. "Hmm, must be the Pepsi-soaked, Cap'n Crunch breakfasts. A sure cure-all," I teased.

He laughed. "Indeed."

Oatmeal diet of my youth, more like it, I thought.

Then I looked down at my lap and frowned. "I'm having more panic attacks, and I'm waking up during the night. It feels like what a defibrillator would feel like—a huge slam to my body. It's interrupting my sleep."

"Induced by stress," he said.

I nodded.

He listened again to my heart and studied me. "Stress."

Yeah, right, I thought. The stress of the lawsuit and the closet monsters. I was silent.

"Any problems with your allergies?"

I shook my head, while he waited patiently for more of any concerns I wished to address. I offered a half-hearted smile, a dismissal, and refused to share further by looking away. Then he stood and smiled. "Okay, Kim, let's take care of you. I'll be right back."

I let out a small breath and realized I hadn't addressed my weight loss to him. Then I looked out the window, brought my finger up to my mouth as if to chew on my nails and remembered: I'd never done such a thing before. To make matters worse I could see black clouds rolling in, threatening storms. I chewed on my lower lip, watching the skies grow darker. Joe always held me tight during storms. I was terrified of them.

The doctor returned shortly with a brown paper bag, pulled out a handful of pill samples, and placed them in my hand.

"This is a new drug for anxiety and depression. Let's give this a try for a month. Take one tablet twice a day." He pushed the bag into my other hand and walked to the door. "Make an appointment to follow up next month." He pointed at me. "Next month, Kim." Then he smiled kindly and slipped out the door.

I sat there, staring at the bag of pills for the longest time. Then, I raised my hand to silence a sob. "I've been reduced to this?"

I scooted off the examining table, grabbed my jacket, walked over to the white metal trash can and popped it open with my foot. Tossing the paper bag and my handful of pills inside the can, I opened the examining room door and made my way back toward the receptionist's area.

A follow-up visit a month later would have my doctor appreciatively high-fiving me for my actions.

But it was today and today's always-silent, never-sharing voice which had my legs jellied, threatening to give way as I walked out of my doctor's office and into a thunderstorm.

When I got home, I changed out of my clothes and into my sweats. I stepped out my door, into a violent storm and ran. I ran for a long time. And I kept running every day until I gained a lead on the monsters and was too exhausted to feel their harsh grip.

Seventeen
The leaky nun

The nun gripped my face with a tight clamp, released it and shoved me back.

"I don't feel so good, Sister Anthony." My face felt like it was on fire. I rubbed my cheeks and stood waiting.

"Who gave you this? It's not a pass." She sneered as I passed along the note.

"Sister Deloris Marie . . . at breakfast. It's from — "

"Get on down to her dorm." She dropped the note on the floor, then turned her back and dismissed me.

With trembling hands, I picked up the note for free passage and headed toward Sister Charlotte's dorm. I found a weary Sister Charlotte waiting in the sterile washroom beside her dog's feeding area. The old nun looked sad. For weeks now, I'd heard the big girls' rumors about Sister Charlotte running through the halls at night, uncontrollably. She claimed she could fly and would flap her arms. I wondered if the witch of my own past nightmares was still lurking.

Nervously, I looked back over my shoulder. I'd also overheard the whispers of some of the nuns. Sister Anthony had huddled with two other nuns. "Sister Charlotte needs to be sent away."

"Her addiction."

"Dry out."

"Tsk, tsk."

No matter how hard I strained my ears, I remained perplexed. The strange words confused me. What needed to dry out? And what was an addiction? I would steal glances at Sister

Charlotte every chance I got. The only exposed areas of Sister Charlotte's body were her hands and face, and they certainly didn't seem to be wet or leaky. I stole another peek at the floor beside Beigy's food dish, where she had just moved. No leaks there. I wrinkled my forehead. What needed to dry out? Maybe if I knew what was wet and leaking on her, I would then know what addiction was.

I stood before Sister Charlotte and waited to hear why I'd been summoned. She reached for my face, felt my forehead with the back of her wrist, then linked her hands behind her back.

"I'll be going away for a while. On retreat." She looked past me.

I understood that all the nuns went on retreat at some point during the year. I didn't know what they did at retreat, only that they would quietly leave for about two weeks once a year and return just as quietly. I searched her face. Her gray eyes were red and watery. I knew Sister Charlotte had just had her retreat less than two months ago. It was much too soon, in my mind.

"I want you to care for Beigy while I'm away. You are nearly eight years old and I believe you can handle this task."

My jaw dropped.

"It's a huge responsibility caring for Beigy. Do you think you can keep up with your duties and this?" She waved her arms like a slow moving, magical wand, and my eyes followed, halfway expecting someone else to come forward and snatch this miraculous gift away from me.

I felt my heart do a flip, then I looked down at the floor. "Yes I will. Er, I can, Sister Charlotte. I'll take care of him good! Real good," I added. I glanced over my shoulder, searched for the witch who had caused all this. That evil witch. It had to be the witch.

"I've written down all my instructions." She handed me a long sheet of paper along with a green paper pass to be given to Sister Anthony. "This pass will give you permission to move freely between dorms."

She walked me out to the hall and I kept my nose to the ground, checking for leaks.

"Thank you, Sister Charlotte." I clutched the papers protectively and gave a small wave. I did a couple of skips down the quiet hall, turned back once to see Sister Charlotte's weak smile and guiltily changed my skip to a walk. Once out of the nun's sight, I was unable to control myself. I skipped and hummed as I moved toward my dorm.

"I am a big girl now! Sister Charlotte thinks so, and she practices medicine, so it must be true." I smiled.

"Wait till I tell Regina." I hugged myself and laughed. "Hmm." Regina was still sick in bed. Two weeks ago she'd gotten something I wanted and didn't have: attention and rest. She'd gotten the mumps. The bumpys, I'd call them. Ever since, she was relieved from all duties. Sister Anthony had even brought food to her bed.

And, that's when I decided: I. Wanted. Regina's. Bumpys.

"Stay away from Regina or you'll catch her mumps. Don't anyone DARE touch her," Sister Anthony had warned.

I'd picked up a smooth, greenish rock on the playground, placed it in my sock and took it to Regina.

"What are you doing Kimmi? I'll tell." Regina turned over in her bed and moaned, "Sister, Sister."

"Shush, Regina Croft." I placed my hand over her mouth.

"This here is a magic rock with healing in it." I put the green rock to her cheek. "Here, I just have to rub it six times in a circle, say the magic words and put it back to my cheek to get your, er, to heal you."

I rolled her over to face me, then I rubbed the rock on her cheek in a circle and started counting. "One. Bumpys be gone." Regina moaned. I put the rock to my cheek and rubbed after each number. "Two. Bumpys be gone." I rubbed harder. "Three. Stop moving, Regina! Four—"

The rock flew out of my hand. Sister Anthony grabbed my arm and twisted it, forcing me to my knees, then threw back her hand and slapped me hard across the mouth.

"Get out of here! NOW!"

I'll tell Regina about Beigy later. I did another skip, looked back to Sister Charlotte's dorm and stopped. My thoughts raced. Doubt crept in. The other nuns didn't like Beigy. Sister Charlotte was the only nun who had the privilege of having a pet. I'd overheard their comments many times. Sister Jean had said just last week, "Sister Charlotte shouldn't have special privileges just because she's a nurse. No one else is allowed a pet."

Would Sister Anthony allow me to run down to the dorm several times a day to care for Beigy? She'd kicked at him just last week in passing. How would I find the time? There were chores, studies, and Mass every morning. Daily afternoon and evening prayers, school. Oh, and the fruit orchards. It was harvest again and we'd be spending many hours picking fruit for the nuns.

Uncertainty and fear erased my brief moment of happiness. I stopped dead in my tracks. What if the witch gives me the leakys and addiction? Or, what if Beigy gets hurt or sick? Worse, what if he keels over? I gasped at the thought. Though I feared Beigy, I feared letting down Sister Charlotte even more.

Three days later, I slouched in the confining wooden church pew, exhausted from days of running between my dorm and Sister Charlotte's. Mass seemed especially long that morning. Only six-fifteen, and there was still thirty-five minutes to go. My head throbbed and it hurt to swallow. To make matters worse, Father Lammers was waving the incense urn around again. The smell was overpowering, and I always had difficulty keeping my stomach settled when the incense was burned.

Why did they have to do this before breakfast? Once I'd actually fainted in the small chapel during the Benediction.

The Latin words were becoming a jumble. Would it ever
end? I squirmed, looked down and tried to concentrate by
counting the freckles on my arm. Useless, I'd done that
hundreds of times. There were still six. I looked up at the altar. I
dared not think of my dammits in God's house. Even though I
couldn't sense God in here, still . . .

I wiped cold sweat off my brow. I wished Father Lammers
would turn around to face his audience. This would signal
Communion, and then it would all end shortly. I blinked hard,
struggled to overcome my dizziness. Squirming, I forced myself
to sit straighter. This earned me a quick pinch on the ear from
Sister Camilla.

I gasped for air, but the claustrophobic chapel, packed full
of nuns and children, provided no relief. Robotically, I repeated
the ever changing kneel, stand, and sit sequence. Miraculously, I
endured it without passing out.

Breakfast was running late. Mass had run over, and Beigy
would have to wait till I came back from the cafeteria. I fretted.

After the cafeteria emptied, I stood fearfully before Sister
Deloris Marie, waiting for her to acknowledge my presence. The
bowl of oatmeal shook in my hand. She finally gave me
permission to speak.

"Sister, please, I'm supposed to go to Sister Charlotte's
dorm."

She scowled. I cowered and took a small step back.

"Beigy hasn't had his morning food yet, I promised Sister
Charlotte."

Sister Deloris Marie grabbed the bowl then delivered a
quick but powerful slap that resonated off the walls. I fell down
awkwardly, cracking my head when I hit the concrete floor.
Then I wet my pants.

A knotted wet bleach rag hit me in the face and fell to the
floor beside me. "Finish this oatmeal, Missy, then floors," she
snapped and shoved the bowl into my hand.

I stuffed three spoonfuls into my mouth, ran over to the garbage can, pretended to scrape my bowl, then spewed the mouthful into the can.

I scrubbed the cafeteria floor quickly and furiously, pausing only to make sure my hands would pass Sister Deloris Marie's cruel test and to glance at the white face of the round institutional clock. Several times I snuck my hands up to my mouth. My tiny, razor-sharp teeth nipped, tore at the flesh on the backside of my hand to draw blood and to hasten the cleaning process. I'd learned this trick from watching the big girls, to pass Sister Deloris Marie's inspection and earn my badge.

My panties were sticky and uncomfortable. I felt miserable. Two and half hours later found me walking out of the cafeteria and nearly running down the empty halls. There was no time to waste.

I walked into Sister Charlotte's dorm. The hair on the nape of my neck stood up. It was quiet. All of her charges had been spread to different dorms throughout the orphanage. I looked carefully around for the witch and instead saw the form of an obese dog standing in the dark hall waiting, looking very much like an overstuffed sausage link.

I flipped the light switch and breathed a heavy sigh of relief. I'd half expected to find him ill or worse since he had waited so long for his breakfast!

Feeling ill myself, I tugged at my soiled panties and cautiously slipped past him and into the washroom. Carefully, I turned on the faucet, held the bowl of stale dry dog food under, removed and counted to twenty to soak, as previously instructed by Sister Charlotte.

The water stung my hands. I blew hard. It didn't help. They were raw and still bleeding from scrubbing Sister Deloris Marie's floors. Afraid, I held the dish out to Beigy. I knew he would growl and snap at me when I sat it in front of him. Usually I was fast, but my reflexes were slow this morning and he nabbed my stinging hand. Tears formed in my eyes and I backed up and stood a respectful distance from his feeding area.

"Hurry, Beigy," I whispered. I kept glancing over my shoulder. "I don't want to get the leakys or addiction. Hurry now!"

Beigy took his time. After he was done, I led him down the back stairwell and outside to do his business. I hugged my stomach to ease the sharp hunger pains. Then I looked over to the dairy barn. The black and white Holsteins moved awkwardly about with bellies fattened from the day's corn silage. They looked so content as they munched on wild grasses.

Looking down, I spotted a patch of sweet clover and wild, sour pickle grass. I bent over and grabbed two fistfuls. My stomach burned raw as I stuffed the grasses into my mouth, chewed and swallowed. I wiped the dirty, grassy remains from my mouth onto the sleeve of my dress, called for Beigy and hurried back up to the dorm.

Before leaving Sister Charlotte's dorm, I moved with caution as I bent down and rubbed the small dog's back. Beigy's dark brown eyes stared up at me without emotion, much like his mistress. I quickly retreated.

I looked up at the washroom clock, felt my soiled panties and worried about being late. One last pet for Beigy, then I rushed out of Sister Charlotte's dorm.

Sister Anthony had said she would show a movie in Sabrina Hall. I'd try and catch up with my dorm later. Though I'd hate to miss the movie, I worried more about the wet panties I was now wearing.

The dorm was quiet as I entered, and I breathed a sigh of relief. I felt my panties and although they were no longer wet, the thought of them soiled disgusted me. I wrinkled my nose and sighed. Whenever I received an unexpected blow, I'd wet my panties and it seemed to be happening a lot lately, both the wetting and the blows.

I only had three panties and washday was two days away. Still, I couldn't wear the soiled panties all day. I thought quickly. Running to my locker, I retrieved the only pair of clean panties I had left. I changed quickly and decided to wash my soiled panties and hang them in my locker to dry.

"Oh, ouch." I sucked air between clenched teeth. The hot water burned my raw hands. I reached for the soap, then was stunned by an unexpected ringing in my ear.

My ear went numb. My fresh panties grew wet. Again.

Sister Anthony towered over me. I could see the faces of my peers peeping curiously from behind the long black robes of the nun.

"Sister Anthony, I'm sorry, Sister. Sister, please, Beigy needed, I needed ... My panties, they got wet ..."

Sister Anthony raised her hand as the sarcastic words dripped from her tongue as she humiliated me in front of my peers. "You belong back in the toddlers' dorm. You are a BIG baby, with no self-control. You need diapers!" To conclude her long tirade of abuse, Sister Anthony snapped at me viciously. "Diapers!"

And adding a pinch of salt to the wound she addressed my peers, taking care to aggressively enunciate each word. She pointed her witchy finger in my face and wagged it. "Since she did not have permission to wash, and since she lacks control, she can spend the rest of her afternoon washing linens." Smirking at me, she continued. "In the meantime I'll be taking my big girls down to watch the Shirley Temple movie."

I hung my head in shame. Standing wearily over the porcelain tub, I began repeatedly washing, rinsing, and wringing sheet after sheet.

I really did love the Shirley Temple movies.

"Dammit," I fumed. My tiny feet stomped the floor, echoing off quiet bare walls.

"Dammit, a hundred times."

You go to Hell when you are bad. I scrubbed furiously on the linens.

I am too a big girl! I really am!

I looked out the third-story window. Night was falling. I fretted and wiped my brow with a bed linen. How many bed linens had I washed? My hands felt as if they were on fire. I fed the last linen into the old washing tub's wooden wringer and cranked.

It had been a long time since my oatmeal-vomit mixed breakfast, lunch had been no more than a passing thought, and my earlier snack of wild grasses had left a burning sensation in my stomach. I surveyed the pile of clean linens I'd placed on the floor. Reaching for the orphans' stool, I climbed up and pinned the linens onto the rope line to dry. I remembered Beigy and ran down the back stairwell to check on him one last time before rushing back to my dorm.

Tired and spent, I walked into the washroom and gathered my gown for bedtime. My heavy sigh betrayed defeat as I changed my clothes.

Ducking, I attempted to walk past Sister Anthony. She hit my face with one last stinging slap. "You're a baby and you belong in the toddlers' dorm!"

I retreated toward my bed and escaped my own living nightmare in dreams of menacing dogs, turning into barreled copies of Chihuahua'd Beigy wolves, and halves of grapefruits topped with beautiful, luscious cherries.

The next morning I woke up with my face on fire. My cheeks felt like bumpy cherries. I couldn't swallow from the pain in my neck and throat.

I'd gotten Regina's bumpys.

Eighteen
The liaison

Sister Anthony slapped my swollen bumpy cheeks. "Get out of that bed, you lazy Injun," she hissed. "You've been laying there for over a week. Point your knees to Satan, then get on downstairs and take care of Beigy. Sister Michael is fed up with taking care of that filthy beast."

She yanked me up by my hair. I cried out.

"God gave you those mumps because you're bad, Missy!"

I climbed out of bed, kneeled down and said my morning prayers before scrambling toward the washroom. I looked at my reflection. My cheeks were red from the nun's slaps. They were still swollen and a little bumpy, but not like the week before. I cupped my hands and poured cold water over them, then I ran down to feed Beigy and hurried to Mass. My energy had returned a little.

I was almost out the cafeteria door when Sister Deloris Marie snatched my collar and boomed, "Floors, Missy!"

Mother Superior caught up with me in the hall two hours later. Yanking me by the ear, she pulled me to her side. "Where have you been? I sent for you over an hour ago."

"Sister Deloris Marie—"

"Wash your face and meet me in Sabrina Hall. There's a visitor waiting for you." She gave another hard yank to my ear and released me.

"Yes, Mother." I sped to Sister Charlotte's dorm, fed Beigy, and washed my face.

I wondered when Sister Charlotte would return. Maybe she was gone forever.

I headed down to the basement of Saint Thomas, winding my way through dark narrow passages to Sabrina Hall. I wondered who my visitor was. Visitors were rare around Saint Thomas.

The elderly lady of fifty-odd years waited patiently. Sitting on a small metal and plastic folding chair against a far wall, she looked like Queen Victoria, or some sort of royalty from the recent Shirley Temple movie.

Her platinum hair had been coiffed into soft, short curls. The expensive-looking powder blue skirt and jacket she wore flattered her small frame. The blue-heeled shoes matched perfectly. A delicate rope of gleaming opalescent pearls hung around her neck.

I grinned as I approached. Mrs. Lindauer stood up and opened her arms. Falling happily into them, I inhaled the sweet scents of lavender and sweet pea. I'd known Mrs. Lindauer all my life, and I adored her. I didn't know how or why she knew me, or why she paid me visits once or twice a year. I was only aware that the rare visits were causes for much joy. I never questioned our relationship and was unaware that it was the obligation of duty that sent her to me.

Mrs. Lindauer was a liaison between the State of Kentucky and Saint Thomas Orphan Asylum-Saint Vincent Orphanage. Taking my hands into her own, she studied them. Noting the dried blood and redness, her eyes were then directed to the new scar near my left eye. She raised her eyebrows and frowned.

Speaking in a whisper, she inquired about my hands. "Do they hurt?"

My nails had once again been cut to the quick for discipline, and the rawness still remained from Sister Deloris Marie's fresh floor cleaning.

"No, Ma'am," I assured her. Uncomfortable, I withdrew my hands from hers and linked them behind my back, shrugging off any further questions.

She stroked my cheek. "I heard you had the mumps? Still look a bit peaked. And a little swollen, I see."

I nodded.

"I'm taking you out for a day visit." She turned and reached for her purse.

I gave a huge smile. "Oh, thank you, Mrs. Lindauer!"

I climbed awkwardly into her tank-sized Pontiac, barely able to contain my excitement. I inhaled the scent of the new leather and rubbed the soft seat. The wide red bench seat enabled me to sit close beside Mrs. Lindauer.

We drove down country lanes with arching canopies of ancient oaks and elms. Mrs. Lindauer rolled down her window. I smelled the sweetness of the pure, fresh country air, mixed with the season's last cut grasses and the promise of an early winter. A cool wind caressed my face with whispered kisses as it randomly tossed about my chopped blonde hair. I got up on my knees, stuck out my tongue to feel its touch.

Mrs. Lindauer laughed, and I plopped back down and smiled. After driving for several miles, making comfortable chat, we came upon a small, busy town. My eyes rapidly devoured the scenery. I was stunned to see all the finely dressed people and children walking about. I pointed, remembered my manners and tucked my hand beneath my bottom. Then I looked down at my faded, brown-checkered dress before bringing my attention back to the view out the window. "Oh, oh look, Mrs. Lindauer. The people! Oh!"

There were dozens of small shops with people scurrying in and out. I couldn't soak it up fast enough. Mrs. Lindauer smiled. Flabbergasted into silence, I sat on my knees and strained my neck to see out the car's window.

Mrs. Lindauer pulled into a lot where a giant ice cream cone was etched onto the storefront's window. I read the words, Ice Cream and Sundries Shoppe.

We entered together, and Mrs. Lindauer placed our order. "I'll have a strawberry ice cream in a cup, and a chocolate on a cake cone." We settled into empty seats by the far window at a freshly cleaned table. I glanced uncertainly out the red-checked, curtained window, then back to my ice cream cone. I looked to Mrs. Lindauer, nervously. What was this, and how should I eat it? Never had I seen anything like it. It was very cold and looked like dark brown slop, and even worse, a little like the oatmeal gruel mix served at the orphanage.

Mrs. Lindauer ate her strawberry serving from a small cup-like bowl with a spoon and seemed to be enjoying it. I looked around anxiously. I didn't have a spoon. Then the ice cream began dripping on my wrist and onto the red Formica table.

I was being bad again and causing a mess. My eyes watered.

"What is it, Kim?" I lowered my head in shamed silence.

I flinched and pulled back when she leaned over the table. Taking the cone gently from my hand, she licked one side of it several times. A dab of chocolate graced her elegant nose. She grinned at me, and I giggled and covered my mouth. Smiling, she handed the cone back. "Go ahead, try it!"

I cautiously took a tiny lick. "It's sweet, like the sugar in the old sugar bucket back at the orphanage!" My eyes widened.

It didn't take long for me to catch up with Mrs. Lindauer. My ice cream disappeared rapidly, and not another drop was wasted on the old table.

Casually, we strolled hand in hand down the block. What a peculiar sight we made, the ragged orphan and the refined lady.

We came upon a shop and Mrs. Lindauer opened the door for me. I caught a glimpse of the words Apothecary Shoppe before entering. I tried to mouth out the words I didn't understand. The busy shopkeeper smiled pleasantly at Mrs. Lindauer but looked suspiciously at me. I offered her a huge grin. Mrs. Lindauer inquired about salves. "I'd like the best ointment for cuts and chafes."

"We have several to choose from. These are two excellent ones." The shopkeeper pushed two round tins toward Mrs. Lindauer and scowled at me. I shrank back.

Mrs. Lindauer picked up the one decorated in roses. "I'll take this tin of Smith's Rosebud Salve."

We left and walked another block through town, passing several storefronts along the way, until we came to a small, park-like setting. Finding a shaded bench, facing the traffic of people, we took a seat. I inhaled deeply and gave Mrs. Lindauer my most appreciative smile.

Looking at the passersby, I grinned when their curious glances made contact. I marveled at the children, especially the little girls around my age. Sporting colorful lace dresses, with brightly colored ribbons adorning their carefully curled hair—they looked to be from a fancy storybook.

"Oh, they are so pretty!" I exclaimed.

"You're very pretty too, Kim!" she said.

I gasped. No one had ever said that to me before.

The children's bright white lacy anklet socks were so pretty! The beautiful shiny black patent leather shoes slapped the sidewalk merrily as they walked, securely holding their mother's hands.

I studied my own shoes and socks. Noting the dingy, torn, plain white socks and the tattered, ugly brown loafers with a quarter-sized hole in the right, I quickly tucked them under the bench.

Still, I smiled as I observed my new surroundings. Interrupting my thoughts, Mrs. Lindauer pulled out her purchase and opened the small tin of ointment. "This will heal your hands." With deliberate gentleness she applied the salve to my hands. The ointment was cool and soothing and provided instant relief.

"Thank you." I said shyly.

She grabbed her pocket book and sat it on her lap. Her face softened as she looked up at me. "Kim, I have a present for you."

Stunned, I gaped up at her. "Oh, me?"

"You're a big girl now, eight years old, and today is your birthday!"

"Oh?" My eyes widened.

She reached into her shiny black pocketbook and retrieved a beautiful small gold box with a tiny curled gold ribbon.

"Happy Birthday, Kim!"

"Happy Birthday, Mrs. Lindauer!"

She laughed, and I joined her.

"Mrs. Lindauer, it's the most beautiful thing I've ever seen!"

"Kim, there is a present inside the box. Open it!"

"Oh?" I wrinkled my brow and turned over the small golden box. I opened it very carefully and stared inside at the beautiful bracelet resting on a puff cloud of cotton. It was set in gold with four scarab stones flanking each side of a center golden bar.

The eight stones were different colors, and I felt their rough texture. Counting them twice, I smiled.

"Mrs. Lindauer, look! The bracelet has eight stones, my favorite number. Number eight!" I held it up to her and counted out for her.

She smiled and measured the bracelet around my wrist, then frowned. "Hmm, a tad big, you'll lose it. I'll just remove a couple of stones." She pulled a coin out of her purse and pried off two beads, then adjusted and secured the bracelet around my wrist.

I laughed. "Now six stones. Jenny's favorite number!"

I peered closely and could see a little bit of my reflection in the narrow gold center bar.

Mrs. Lindauer patted my hand. "What is your birthday wish, Kim?"

I was puzzled.

"On birthdays you're allowed to make one wish."

"Oh. One?"

She nodded.

Getting excited, I leaned forward to reveal my wish.

"A forever family, that's what I want! That's what I'd mostly wish for. When does the wish come true, Mrs. Lindauer? It's okay, I can wait a little if it takes awhile. I'm a big girl."

Mrs. Lindauer sat quiet as I patiently explained in detail to her. "Just like in the Shirley Temple movies! I want a mother and father! And a family that I can have forever—a forever family! Do you think I'm too big of a big girl now?"

Mrs. Lindauer eye's clouded and she looked away. I happily chattered on. I asked, "Maybe you could be my forever family, my mother? I will try very, very hard to be good, and you can punish me when I'm bad, or whenever you like. And I hardly ever cry when I get a beating, but if I do, I'd do it quietly. And I can wash linens and clothes very, very good. I scrub floors and can even care for dogs." I nodded my head. "Why even Sister Charlotte thinks I'm a big girl!"

I took a small breath and paused, trying to decide whether or not to tell Mrs. Lindauer about the oatmeal.

You go to Hell when you are bad.

Mrs. Lindauer's eyes watered and she looked away. Staring off into the distance, she pulled a lacy monogrammed hanky out of her bulky pocketbook and dabbed at her eyes.

My smile faded.

Not looking at me, Mrs. Lindauer stood up. "It's time to go."

Climbing into the Pontiac Bonneville, I stared out the window. I worried about the oatmeal and the oatmeal tears, that Mrs. Lindauer didn't want a bad girl like me. She must know I was bad. I fought back the well that threatened to overflow.

We were quiet on the long trip back to Saint Thomas. Pulling into the huge circular drive, Mrs. Lindauer parked the car. With tenderness she applied one more layer of ointment onto my hands. Mrs. Lindauer looked concerned. "There is a family I want you to visit this August."

I gasped. "My wish! So soon?"

"You would stay with the family for a while. Would you like that?"

I smiled, nodded yes. A million questions went unanswered, but I remained quiet. My hand shook as I held up my wrist to Mrs. Lindauer. "The bracelet is yours to keep, Kim."

I shook my head. "I have to take it off. It's not allowed and it'll be taken away."

She unfastened the clasp, raised her eyebrow and put it in my hand. She curled my fingers around it. "You keep it, Kim." She gave my hand a small squeeze and released it.

Any gifts received were quickly confiscated by the nuns, never to be seen again. The only possessions you owned were the clothes on your back, and they were only borrowed, never owned. They could be taken at any time and given to another orphan or magically disappear.

Mrs. Lindauer hugged me good-bye. A sob escaped, racking my body. I pulled away, quick to offer her a smile. I tried to hide my sadness.

Bending down, I carefully tucked the beautiful scarab bracelet deep within my thin sock, to hide from the nuns. I slid across the smooth bench seat and reached for the car latch, stopping to look back at Mrs. Lindauer one last time before I climbed out of the car.

Taking a small gulp, I turned once to wave a small good-bye, then I headed into the dismal building and back into Saint Thomas's arms.

Nineteen
An invitation to a funeral

I walked out of the gloomy building and ran toward the McCreary cottage. Saint Thomas's groundskeepers lived in the quaint cottage, nestled amongst scattered tall pines, just beyond the girls' playground. I would stare longingly at the tidy home, with its picket fence border. It looked like something out of a storybook. The scent of wild honeysuckle intertwined in the fencerow was like an invitation to a sweet idyll inside. I'd never been inside, but my imagination ran rampant with fancy settings.

I'd known the McCreary's since my early arrival at Saint Thomas. Like everything else at the orphanage, they were a timeless reminder of permanent existence, which stood perpetually still. They had no children that I knew of, but kept a collie named Lassie and an old gray tomcat named Smokey. I'd often wonder what it would be like to wake each morning in that cheery cottage rather than the cold, sterile building I occupied.

In early spring, Mrs. McCreary would plant a bountiful flower and vegetable garden. She breathed life into her landscape with gloriously painted palm-sized zinnias, pink coral-bells, sweet-smelling lavender, evening primrose and cupid's dart. Each year she would add more, putting to shame the finest of her pictorial English garden books, which she shared with me on occasion. Why, even in the dead of winter, she was able to coax the tiny jonnie-jump-ups to endure the inclement weather.

She taught me some of the names of the flowers, adding more to my flora vocabulary each year. Occasionally, Mrs. McCreary would wave and offer a smile to us when we were on the playground.

Once during a long cold snap, she had Mr. McCreary build a small bonfire between the playground and her cottage for us. Then, Mrs. McCreary came over and handed out freshly baked buttery snickerdoodles and crisp ginger snaps to ease our cold and hunger.

My bare feet were numb, red as ripe cherries from standing so long on the playground's icy ground. My bluish hands shook as I reached for a cookie off Mrs. McCreary's tray. The scent of fresh ginger made my mouth water. I hesitated. I couldn't decide whether to hold the cookie to warm my hands or eat it, to still the angry rumbles of my empty stomach. A stab of hunger pain cramped my stomach. I doubled over and Regina took advantage and knocked the warm ginger snap right out of my hand. I bent to retrieve it, but it was too late. Regina crushed it into the icy-slushed ground with her large, filthy foot.

I knelt down on the cold ground, scrambled for the cookie remains, then stuffed the scattered, dirty ice-mixed crumbs into my mouth. When I finished eating, I felt colder and hungrier than before I'd started. My knees stung from the scraping of flesh against ice. I blew on my knees, wiped the bloodied and cracked skin with the hem of my dress and glared at Regina. She smirked back.

I searched Mrs. McCreary's cookie tray. Empty. My eyes followed as she walked away.

Lassie barked and I turned, then laughed when he chased an old pickup truck barreling down the dirt-lined road next to our playground. The truck veered off the road and brushed up against the branches of barren cherry trees that flanked it. It swerved several times to miss the collie. Puffs of frosted dirt clouds coiled around dog and truck. Finally, Lassie hit his mark by popping a tire, a life-long habit. The truck screeched to a halt and the visiting worker jumped out. He yelled, waved his arms angrily in the air, then kicked the damaged tire in frustration.

Old Smokey rubbed against my leg as I watched. I reached down and scratched his chewed-up ears. "You've been over at that ol' dairy barn again, Smokey. Those wild barn cats are going to kill you one day."

"Smokey's dead," announced Mr. McCreary. He took off his cap, rubbed his bald head. It was early afternoon, and Mr. McCreary stood at the gate of the picket fence with his wife. The sun beat down and reflected off Mrs. McCreary's straw-sequined hat she'd made in the spring. She covered her mouth to stifle a cry. Mr. McCreary gave her a small embrace, then walked away.

Mrs. McCreary gestured toward me to come to the fence. Obediently, I scurried forward. The other girls followed.

"Smokey's been found dead about a quarter-mile down the dirt road. I need your assistance to retrieve the body. Would you girls like to help?" She took off her straw hat and fanned her face with it.

We all raised our hands.

"Thank you," she said, giving us an appreciative smile. "I'll need everyone's help. I'll just go and get Jane." She walked to the back of her cottage. A few minutes later, she came back, pulling an old wooden Janesville wagon behind her. It was filled with a bucket of flowers, plastic and several small hand shovels.

"Regina, Camilla, you stay behind and dig the grave over there." She pointed to the tall white pine behind her cottage, then handed each of them a shovel. She lifted the bucket from the wagon. "Anna, take this and put it near the pine."

"Yes, Ma'am," Anna answered softly.

Jane's metal wheels squeaked as we walked silently down the road.

Flies buzzed around the smashed, dead cat. Mrs. McCreary handed out small pieces of plastic to me and three other girls. My stomach churned as we lifted the blood-soaked, furry Smokey and put him into the wagon. I swallowed back the lock in my throat, took a huge breath, then held it, trying my hardest not to breathe.

Mrs. McCreary led the procession back to the gravesite.

The three girls' faces were sweaty from digging the grave. And I suppressed a giggle when I saw Regina's red hair plastered to her head like a dead fly on sticky paper. I whispered in her ear as I passed, "Tut, tut, tut, somebody looks like a dried-up ol' strawberry." Then I flicked her forehead as I casually sauntered by, arching my brow in challenge. Regina rubbed her always-sunburned face. Her pale green eyes darkened then shot daggers at me. Her yellow freckles looked as if they'd pop right off, like hot dancing grease on a griddle. I smiled back sweetly.

Mrs. McCreary walked over and peered into Smokey's final resting spot, nodded, then took her hands and scooted two large piles of dirt to its side. "Good job, girls." She sniffed loudly and wiped away her tears, painting her cheek with dirty streaks with each swipe. My heart exploded. It hurt to see her cry. Mrs. McCreary was so sad. I looked away, felt a tear of my own escape down my cheek and rubbed it quickly away. We stood quietly beneath the tall shaded pine behind the cottage and waited for her instruction.

"Gather up some dirt, line up and put it in Smokey's grave."

I picked up a handful of the rich Kentucky soil and crumbled it slowly into Smokey's open grave. "I'll miss you, Smokey." I stepped back toward the trunk of the pine as others moved forward to fill his grave with scoops of dirt.

Mrs. McCreary stood over his grave. "Let's form a circle, girls. Psalm 23. The Lord is my —"

We stepped forward, bowed our heads and joined in. " — shepherd, I shall not want."

After the prayer Mrs. McCreary reached into the gallon bucket and handed us each a painted daisy from her garden. We followed behind her as she circled around the cat's grave, then she placed a flower on top of the mound of soil.

Three days later I knelt under a sprawling sugar maple on the playground. I made sure nobody was looking then I dug for my scarab bracelet. To keep the nuns from taking it, I'd buried it on the playground. I'd been digging it up and reburying it in different spots to keep it safe, and now I couldn't find it. I looked over my shoulder. Thankfully the nuns rarely stayed on the playground, they'd just poke their heads out a door every now and then and holler something that no one understood. Tears and sweat blended and I wiped my face, leaving it mud-streaked. I looked up, saw a tall scraggly pine, and remembered I'd buried it there. I ran to the tree, clawed the dirt with my hands, and sobbed with relief when I saw the gold of the bracelet shine through. Then I heard Mrs. McCreary call for the others and me.

"Kim, get over here, quick-like! Girls, girls!"

I quickly reburied the bracelet, wiped my face with the sleeve of my dress and ran toward her fence.

Excited, Mrs. McCreary recounted her story to the growing number of girls who leaned across the picket fence to listen. "I awoke to loud mews outside my cottage this morning," she said breathlessly. "I opened the door, and oh-lawsey, you could have knocked me over with a feather! I looked down and found a very hungry and very demanding Smokey. Mercy, mercy sakes-alive girls, it seems we buried one of the Thompson cats!" She covered her mouth and smothered a chuckle.

Jaws dropped and gasps echoed.

The Thompsons' cat was one of many. It belonged to a neighboring farm family. Happily, Mrs. McCreary informed us of the cleverness of cats' nine lives. "Cats' lives are shorter because they work hard for their keep. That's why God rewards them with nine lives."

She went back into her cottage, then returned shortly with a plateful of rich butter cookies and a half-gallon, yellow Mason fruit jar filled with sweet tea. We took a huge swig of the sugary liquid, passed it around, then grabbed a cookie off her plate.

I leaned back against the trunk of the tree, broke off a chunk of cookie and bit into it absently. Regina sneered and pointed at my face. "Dirty wild Injun!" she screeched. I ignored her. Instead, I contemplated Mrs. McCreary's words while studying my raw, chapped hands. Although I was only eight, my hands looked as old as Sister Charlotte's. I raised my head, cupped my hands to shield my eyes from the sun, and stared toward the road leading out of the orphanage.

Maybe if I work hard enough, my life will be shorter.

Twenty
Define happy

2005

It felt like I'd put in a hard day's work of grueling labor. I was sapped, completely worn out from the deposition and ready to go home.

The attorneys were wrapping it up. The archdiocese's attorney looked as I felt: spent and about to hit a brick wall.

He straightened his crooked tie, smoothed down his wrinkled jacket and told the court reporter he had no more questions. Someone came forward and removed my microphone.

"Off the record." The attorney sat up straighter and tried to kick it once more by firing off a final successive string of questions and statements.

I crossed my arms and waited for the attorney's silence, his pause. A slow fury stirred inside me, feeding off each pause.

"Do you blame the Church, or the priest and nuns of Saint Thomas, for your sister Pamela's untimely and tragic death?" He arched a brow. Waited.

She's dead and you silenced her in concrete. Dead. A concrete angel presiding over a lone graveyard. Don't speak her name. I tightened my mouth.

"Do you blame the Church, or the priest and nuns of Saint Thomas, for your own anxieties?"

Silence.

"Do you blame the Church, or the priest and nuns of Saint Thomas, for your sister Gayla's destructive life?"

"Do you blame the Church, or the priest and nuns of Saint Thomas, for not adopting you out?"

"Do you blame the Church or priest and nuns of Saint Thomas for Caity's cancer?"

With my fists clenched, I inhaled and waited for him to end. The attorney rambled on for a few minutes, theatrically posing the questions to me. He finally finished, raised his brows, and waited for me to respond.

Silence, like the sound between the cold click of a gun's hammer before the explosive exit of a metal ball. I shook my head and ran my fingers through my tousled hair. "Yes," I practically yelled. Although deep within my heart, I knew some of the answers were no. After all, one did possess free will. So I'd been taught. However, all things given, said, and done, I strongly believed that the seeds had been planted long ago by this controlling religious society. And like an evil weed spreading its roots, it had constantly threatened to strangle and consume, with only the strongest of the strong surviving, eradicating its hold.

A small brown manila folder lay before me. It contained thirty-three one-sided pages. I counted the copied pages and quickly recounted them again for affirmation. I looked up at the attorneys, perplexed, looked down and again scanned the file, consuming its contents. I shook my head as if to will it away. I was rendered speechless. The pages were badly photocopied. It looked to be someone's chicken-scratched diary, not official records. Most of the words were illegible, missing, smeared, and jumbled. I was stunned.

These were my records, submitted by the archdiocese of Louisville, official documents of my entire youth from Saint Thomas-Saint Vincent Orphan Asylum, which my attorney had requested. All summed up in a thirty-three-page joke?

The small file included me *and* my three sisters. Our journeys, our lives from start to end at Saint Thomas-Saint Vincent Orphan Asylum. "My whole youth compressed into a thirty-three-page file, which I share with my three sisters?" I shook my head. "Impossible! My three-year-old dog's veterinarian record is larger than this. Where are the medical records? I certainly received enough medicine for a dozen children's lifetimes."

My mind raced. Suspiciously I wondered, *cover-up?* "Who was supplying all that medicine to the orphans, and more importantly, why and what were all the medicines I had been given?"

I looked across the conference table to the nun and met no challenge.

They said time healed everything, but I was still waiting. I tapped further into my mind. There was something more sinister here. Drug experimentation on orphans no one wanted?

I thought about The Monster Study, a stuttering experiment conducted by scientists of the University of Iowa decades ago; their scientists taught orphans to stutter for speech pathology studies. The truth was exposed in 2001. My stomach knotted. The possibilities were endless.

Innocently, the representatives of the Sisters of Charity and the archdiocese of Louisville professed, "Most of the records had been lost or no longer existed."

"Certainly convenient for them!"

Surprised? I really shouldn't be, I thought.

"For decades I'd been unsuccessful in trying to obtain my records. You said there were none!"

Some things never changed. The Sisters of Charity and the Church were still withholding the full meal, distributing only the disgusting oatmeal gruel mix. How could that be? The Catholic Church, one of the best record keepers in the world? *Ah.* And also one of the most secretive, and who knew how to keep secrets all too well.

I picked up a page, an official copied document that showed the grading of an orphan--me. It marked my childhood interaction with a visiting family. I winced and felt the scalding-hot blush of disgrace creep up and spread across my face. The document, no different from the others, was smeared and largely illegible.

However, I could plainly see the check in one section that leapt from the page like a red flag. *A solitary bad mark.* And how well I'd remembered that mark—that day—the guilt and the shame of receiving the painful beating, along with the exclusion of my *good* checks. I had been mortified. The family with whom I'd shared a weekend visit had given me the *bad* check mark. It seems I had been too demanding for attention. Imagine that—an "it," as Father Lammers refers to me in the document—an orphan, a child, wanting attention, just wanting to be loved *like anyone else.*

Tears of rage mingled with humiliation and threatened to spew.

The male attorney spoke, interrupting my thoughts—grounding me. "Happy?"

I swallowed back my rage, my embarrassment. What was left behind was a bitter aftertaste of hostility. Still reeling from the shock of receiving my personal records, I said, "Excuse me?"

"Are you happy with your life?" He drummed his pencil impatiently on the table.

It took me a minute to respond. I was strangling on the word. Incredulously, I looked at them as well as my own attorney. I tried to process the word, happy. The thought was mind-blowing. *When you stole my tears, you stole my voice, my innocence.*

It was all I could do to check myself and keep from delivering both barrels, blasting the moronic idiot. I was about to lose it, and I never lost it. Was he being sarcastic?

I opened my mouth to reply but closed it, instead swallowing the anger. He wanted to feed off my outrage. He was trained to provoke.

Kick it to the curb, Kim, and let it roll like a runaway hubcap. I chewed on my lower lip and placed my trembling hands in my lap. "Do you mean, am I happy with my current life, my family, or happy that I survived the cruel horrors of the life you subjected me to? Am I supposed to be happy?" I innocently cocked a brow and offered a phony, saccharine smile.

The attorneys looked flustered as they prepared to close the deposition.

The nun looked away and papers were shuffled. My fury heightened, raged, like the silent fracture between the boom of thunder and a wicked crack of lightning.

Leaning over the conference table, the male attorney looked directly into my cold green eyes. "Off the record," he said evenly, "you know we did try to adopt you out? Your mother would never allow it."

Another slap. It hurt, and I could feel my cheek flame red. My mind snapped as the smart shocked my entire being. I gritted my teeth and words exploded like a mouthful of Pop Rocks candy mixed with Pepsi. "Lies! Not true! I was your responsibility, your duty!" My eyes threatened to tear. "You were given complete control by the State of Kentucky, and you chose to immorally map my destiny." I leaned in. "And you tried?" I whispered.

Loud silence.

With a forged, calm composure, I moved in closer. My voice turned cold. "You had a duty. A duty to protect, and you did a lousy job. You should have tried harder."

Kim's Orphan Grading Document

Date: *Aug 3, 1965*

TO: *[handwritten illegible]*

FROM: Rt. Rev. Monsignor H. J. Lammers
Director of Catholic Charities Agency

SUBJECT: To evaluate the adjustment of this child to family life

CHILD: *[handwritten illegible]*

The purpose of the Family Sharing Plan is to prepare the child for family and community living. In answering these questions you are helping us to improve our preparation of children for living outside of the institution. The information should indicate where the child has made a satisfactory family adjustment or where the child was considered unsatisfactory in your home.

If you prefer you may telephone the Agency worker rather than filling out the questionnaire. You have my assurance that the information given will not be used to punish the child, but only to improve our training program designed to prepare institutional children for family living.

1. Did the child happily accept foster family life? Yes ✓ No _____

2. Did the child get along with other children in the home and in the neighborhood?   Yes _____ No _____

3. How did child accept correction?   Well ✓ Badly _____

4. Did the child show approved habits at the table? Yes ✓ No _____

           In personal appearance? Yes ✓ No _____

           In matters of politeness? Yes ✓ No _____

5. Would you consider this child too demanding?

           1. For attention   Yes ✓ No _____

           2. For personal gifts   Yes _____ No ✓

           3. For entertainment   Yes _____ No ✓

6. Did the child speak of its own family?   Yes ✓ No _____

7. Did child show any conduct that should be brought to our attention? Yes _____ No _____

Please return in enclosed envelope at your earliest convenience.

Thanks.

REMARKS: *[handwritten illegible]*

Twenty-one
Praise the lord and pass the ammunition

I spotted a lone horse standing beside a board fence in the distance. I sat on my hands, trying my hardest not to jump up and hang out the car's window. Mrs. Lindauer drove slowly by and I kicked my thin legs up and down nervously, then quickly pressed my face against the car window to stare. "That's a pretty horse, Mrs. Lindauer." I watched as it faded in the distance. "Mrs. Lindauer, what's the name of the family, again?"

"Bernard."

I was having second thoughts about spending time away from my three sisters and the orphanage. I worried about the family I'd soon meet. I glanced at Mrs. Lindauer, but her reassuring smile didn't temper my growing fear, or calm the fluttering butterflies in my stomach.

True to her word, after my eighth birthday, Mrs. Lindauer had come back for me in August.

"Mrs. Lindauer, there's a whole bunch of flying butterflies in my tummy." I poked at my stomach.

Mrs. Lindauer reached over and patted my hand. "We'll be there shortly. The Bernards are anxious to meet you."

I smiled up at her then looked out the window, taking no notice of the fertile farmlands we passed. I was preoccupied with my thoughts and my doubts. I wanted my forever family, but what about my sisters, and what if this wasn't the family and Mrs. Lindauer didn't come back? Who would come and get me, and would my sisters still be at Saint Thomas when I returned?

We pulled onto a gravel road, parked, and climbed out of the car. Mrs. Lindauer bent over, gave me a hug and walked back to her car. I stared up at the farmwoman and swallowed air.

Mrs. Bernard had a medium frame and large bones. Her weather-beaten face and rough, large hands spoke farm wife, though she was a woman of only thirty-some years. Life on the farm had clearly taken its toll. Her small eyes revealed mistrust. Her long auburn hair twisted into aberrant curls that swung freely as she moved. Wearing bright red lipstick smeared thickly upon her lips, she looked like a clownish scarecrow.

I ran back toward the safety of Mrs. Lindauer's Bonneville and clutched the car handle desperately. Mrs. Lindauer's gentle hands pushed mine away. "It's only a short visit, Kim. Go on."

Mrs. Bernard's rough hands tugged me back toward the large Bedford stone ranch house. With my heart racing, I watched as Mrs. Lindauer's car drove out of sight. Mrs. Bernard walked me inside, past the living room, which she made clear was strictly off-limits, and down a narrow hall to a small, dimly lit room.

She gave me a new name. Girl.

"Girl, you'll be sharing the room with my two foster children." She shoved me inside. The tiny room was devoid of color. Two heavy homemade wooden bunk beds consumed the entire area. An ugly brown lamp sat on a crude white table.

"I will not tolerate any trouble from you, Girl." She wagged her finger in front of my face. "I'm not getting paid enough for your long visit."

I shot her a puzzled look, and she answered with a stinging slap. Without missing a beat, she went on to outline a long and detailed list of chores for which I was responsible.

"After dinner, I'll take you and the foster girls to church. Later, I'll walk you around the farm and start you on your chores. In the meantime, find the cellar and bring up the five buckets filled with cabbages. I'm preparing coleslaw for the church tomorrow."

She walked out of the room and I followed. A tall, blonde boy stopped in front of her. His face was oily and pocked full of pimples. "This is my son, Ray, he's a senior this year." She reached up and playfully tousled his hair. He ducked around her, grinned and gave my bottom a sharp pinch.

"Ouch!" I glared at him.

That evening I sat at the round kitchen farm table feeling lost and scared. I worried about my sisters. This family didn't feel right to me, but I didn't know why. I tucked my left hand under my bottom and looked at all the staring faces.

Lisa, a fourteen-year-old foster child, and her sister, four-year-old Susan, sat on opposite sides of me. Seated across from me was Ray, the Bernards' only son, whom I'd taken a quick dislike to earlier in the hall. I squirmed, uncomfortable from their stares.

Mr. Bernard sat directly across from his wife. He was a huge man with a balding head. He rarely spoke, but when he did, his voice was so soft that I had trouble understanding him.

Mrs. Bernard placed her elbows on the table, fisted her hands, and lowered her head. "Bless this food and the hands that prepared it. Bless these sinners as they eat this dinner. Guide and direct us." Everyone said, "Praise the Lord" followed by, "Amen" and supper began.

I looked down at my plate of fried chicken, butter beans and cornbread. The scents were strong and inviting.

With her mouth full and grease smeared across her cheeks, Mrs. Bernard waved a chicken leg in the air. "Eat," she commanded. "Eat, Girl! Long time 'til breakfast." She pointed the chicken leg at me and raised a penciled brow. Unsure, I watched the others hold their chicken. I'd never had such food. I smelled it and took a small cautious bite and then another. My face widened into a huge grin. I looked happily at Mrs. Bernard. She reached over, cackled, and slapped me good-naturedly on the head. Although startled, I laughed back.

Mrs. Bernard passed me some delicious-smelling bread and pointed at a plate of butter to accompany it. I ate every bite on my plate until my tummy ached with the unfamiliar feeling of being full, and I found it difficult to walk to the sink to help with dishes.

The Bernards' church was different from the quiet rhythms of the only church I knew, the Catholic Church. The carnival-like atmosphere shocked me beyond belief. There was loud singing and sudden eruptions of screaming *Amen* and *Praise the Lord* accompanied by dancing and swaying.

My brain whirled. I took a huge gulp and looked around. The priest was called a Brother. With a puffed out chest, he strutted throughout the small country church, loudly cockcrowing his sermon. There were no soft Latin chants, no robes. I felt my eyes go milk-saucer wide when he faced his audience and interacted with exaggerated animation.

The Brother swaggered toward me, lifted me out of the pew and pulled me up to the pulpit. He put his hands on my shoulder and faced me toward the congregation. "Declare yourself, sinner! Ask for His forgiveness, for only then can you be cleansed and walk beside Him."

I flinched at his loud words. He waved to the audience and I shrank back against him. "Let us pray for this sinner." He gripped my shoulders tighter. There was nowhere to run or hide. I felt a hot blush creep up, spread across my face and burn my ears.

Everyone yelled *Praise the Lord* repeatedly.

Then without warning, the Brother dunked my head into the large basin of water beside the pulpit. Dripping wet and horrified, my tears were thankfully hidden.

All this, and today was only my first day. I climbed up to the top bunk bed and cried myself to sleep.

With each passing day, my forever family grew more twisted and violent. Mrs. Bernard was loud, demanding and abrasive.

Quick to deliver slaps, she would shake the foster girls and me like rag dolls. One minute would find Mrs. Bernard laughing and the next erupting like a volcano, spewing out harsh, aggressive words. Madness and chaos prevailed, and the tiniest of hiccups would set her off.

Still I held out hope for this forever family, holding on to hope one minute only to find it shattered within the next.

Weeks passed slowly, as the summer sizzled and matched the household's heated violence. It was my turn to pick the blackberries today. The large, weathered basket bumped off my shins as I followed Mrs. Bernard to the backfield. Sweating in silence, I picked the blackberries alongside a red-faced Mrs. Bernard.

The air was solid and I fanned myself with my hand. Occasionally I would sneak a peek to my left. The trees shaded and arched over a running brook, which gurgled with the refreshing sound of moving water. Oh, how I longed to dip my feet into its coolness and splash the water onto my face. Instead, I frowned and wiped the sweat from my brow and cracked lips with the back of my free hand.

Reaching into the thick bramble, I drew back in pain as the wicked thorns drew blood.

Mrs. Bernard suddenly stopped, smacked my head, and pointed out a very large turtle lying to the left of my basket. "Girl, run quickly and get the heavy galvanized tub."

I ran and awkwardly delivered the big old tub at her feet. Then she placed the tub over the large turtle. Satisfied, she stepped back. "I'll cook it for tomorrow's supper."

I stared at her in horror. "Oh no, Ma'am," I protested. "You're not going to kill him, Mrs. Bernard?"

She delivered a slap. "Get back to work."

Hours passed before she released me from my duties and ordered me to clean up for church services. After returning from church that evening, I joined the foster sisters in their bedroom. Less than a minute later, Mrs. Bernard banged open our bedroom door. Startled, we all retreated toward the far wall and cowered. She rushed me. Yanking me by the hair, Mrs. Bernard dragged me out the door, down the hall, and delivered me to Mr. Bernard, who was waiting in the kitchen.

She screamed, "The turtle is gone; someone has stolen it!" Then she pointed an accusing finger at me.

My eyes widened in disbelief. I'd long forgotten about the captured turtle. With the beginning of a sob, I denied having set the turtle free. "I'm sorry, Mrs. Bernard. I didn't. I wouldn't."

"Shut up, you wicked sinner." She bared her teeth and growled. Then she brought her hand back in a pitcher's stance and backhanded me. I stumbled and fell back against the kitchen table. Sobbing, I shook my head repeatedly. "No, please, I'd never do that. Please."

Mr. Bernard meekly stepped forward to defend me. "Such a huge turtle could have easily lifted up the edge of the tub and crawled away. The girl—"

Mrs. Bernard pushed her husband aside and yanked me forward. Pulling out a bristle hairbrush, she jerked my panties down and delivered blow after blow until she was breathing heavily and had exhausted herself.

Less than a week later, still healing from the previous beating, I was once again unjustly accused of stealing from Mrs. Bernard. This time it was postage stamps. She yanked hard on my hair until she brought me to my knees. "I've never touched a postage stamp. I don't know what—"

She used her fist on me this time. "Repent, you wicked girl. Repent!"

Sobbing between words, I begged for her mercy. "Please, no, please. I beg you, Mrs. Bernard." Two brutal concrete blows to the face had me cowering on the floor, cradling my head and shaking in terror. My panic-stricken tears splattered on the hardwood as my bladder let loose, spilling its contents onto the floor. My tears blended with the urine puddles.

Mrs. Bernard looked down at me. Her eyes narrowed, revealing disgust as she pulled the bristle hairbrush from the large pocket of her apron. And I recoiled not from the brush but from the hatred that spilled out. She used the spiky brush on my face and my body.

"Admit it, you demon!" she screamed.

Blood dripped from my cheek, mixing with drops from my mouth, and my wails of denial drifted through homespun curtains, out the open windows, and blended into lethargic winds, finally alerting Mr. Bernard.

"Stop it, Margaret." His breathing was heavy and a huge sweat spot covered the front of his blue-checked shirt. "Margaret, Margaret!" He took off his cap and wiped his brow. "Stop! You'll kill the girl."

"The sinner stole my stamps. They're gone!"

I made a slow crawl toward the door.

"No, they're in the car, Margaret!" Quickly, he turned, ran to his car and retrieved the forgotten postage stamps, which his wife had left in the glove box.

She kicked me in the side. I screamed and quickly cradled my waist.

"Where'd you put the stamps?" Spit sprayed out of her mouth.

I could only shake my head and gasp for air. She raised her foot. Mr. Bernard blocked the second kick by stepping in front of her. He dangled the stamps in the air in front of his wife to gain her attention. "Look, Margaret, here's the stamps. See?"

She blinked, backed up, and squinted her eyes. Somewhere the faint ticking of a clock could be heard, increasing in volume, and a million minutes passed frozen. The clock's ticks pounded in my ears.

The heartbeat of a terror-stricken child.

Again, Mr. Bernard waved the stamps in front of his wife. Instead of taking them, she pushed his hand aside, bent over me and smacked me hard across the face. I didn't move. I tried not to breathe.

Panting heavily, Mrs. Bernard stepped back, snatched the forgotten stamps from her husband's hand, and ran to her bedroom, leaving behind an echo of her hysterical tears.

Mr. Bernard looked at me as if to speak but instead turned and walked out the door. A few seconds later, I heard the hum of his tractor. Defeated, I rose from the floor and walked painfully to the bedroom. The physical and emotional pain was too much, and I couldn't find the strength to change into my gown for bed. I reached up and wiped at my silent tears. My eyes widened, and horror washed over me as I stared at the blood on my hand that came from the wipe. I was terrified to leave the room to go wash it off my face. I crawled up the ladder of the bunk bed and waited for the sweet reprieve of sleep.

I pulled the bed covers tightly over me. The summer night was hot and sticky, and the stifling air was mixed obnoxiously with the smell of rancid lard from an earlier fried supper. Still, my sweat was cold and smelled of fear. Shaking, I clung even more tightly to the covers.

I could barely get out the beginning of my nightly prayer. "Now I lay me down to sleep, I pray the Lord my soul to keep. If I should die before I wake, please give Mrs. Bernard all my birthday cake."

As the aggression against me increased, I soon summoned my nightly prayer during the days as well, hoping it would shield me from Mrs. Bernard.

August soon faded, and for the first time in my life, I found myself boarding a yellow school bus. I was scared, but I welcomed the freedom from the Bernards' violent home and especially the brief absence of Mrs. Bernard's brutal wrath. Staring silently out the window, I ignored the rude stares, pointing and whispers of the other children. It seems the Bernards' son, Ray, had generously detailed my life to the neighboring farm children.

"Orphan girl! I told 'em. I told 'em, I had an orphan staying at my house."

When I arrived at the school I was shocked to find it so large. There were so many classrooms. With an adult's assistance, I entered a large and very noisy classroom.

The teacher did not wear the nuns' garb. The teacher yelled, "Take your seats!" The children's voices grew louder. "Bell in three minutes. Detention!" She threatened. And the teacher's lack of control scared me.

Each passing day grew noisier and more uncomfortable for me, but I easily adjusted to the schoolwork, as I'd been taught the familiar lessons in the previous years at the orphanage. In this I took comfort, focusing on my studies as a distraction from life with the Bernards.

After two weeks had passed, I still hadn't found a friend at the school. I hung my head and shuffled slowly down narrow halls to reach my classroom. I cowered against the metal lockers more than once when hurrying students rudely bumped me and snickered, "Orphan."

Settling in my school desk, I reached into my used satchel. I frowned. I'd forgotten something but couldn't pinpoint what it was. Pulling out my homework papers, I set them on my desk. Sitting silently in the classroom, I awaited instruction. Then the teacher said, "Get out your science book."

Frantic, I crushed and scattered papers as I searched for my book. It should be here. It should—

I raised my hand. "My book is in my locker, Ma'am."

She nodded. "Retrieve it at once."

Feeling uncomfortable, I walked the narrow, dim corridors to my locker at the other end of the building. Alone in the eerily quiet hallways, I kept looking over my shoulder until I reached my locker. I was trembling. I failed at my first few attempts to open the metal door and couldn't keep from glancing over my shoulder each time I failed. Finally, I got the combination right and dug through my meager belongings for my science book. A tap on my shoulder sent a cold chill down my neck and startled me into dropping my book. I whirled around and felt the blood draining from my face. A violent shiver shook my body.

Standing close to me was a young boy about my age and height. My eyes met his and locked. He stuttered, and my heart pounded rapidly.

"G-girl, y-you're p-p-pretty."

I looked wildly around for help.

Again he stuttered. "G-girl, y-you're p-p-pretty.

I looked into his hazel eyes. I opened my mouth but my voice froze in a silent scream. This boy's presence felt dangerous and I didn't know why. I was so scared I couldn't breathe, then blackness threatened and I struggled to focus. I clenched my fists, turned my face to the locker and lowered my head to cool metal to draw strength. The cold against my skin brought back function and full panic set in.

I yelled, "Go away!"

He tapped my shoulder. Twisting back again, I gasped. He was gone. My heart pounded. Scanning the lengths of the corridors, I found them empty. Shaking, fighting for breath I slammed the locker shut. I picked up my book, dropped it two more times and ran.

The morning classes felt surreal. I felt like I was floating. Lunch was no consolation for my worries, as I'd lost my appetite. My hands shook as I tried to hold my sandwich. I couldn't forget the boy who stood at my locker, and my eyes searched the crowded cafeteria. Trembling, I stood up from the table and discarded my uneaten cheese sandwich into the nearest garbage can.

The ring of the final school bell brought little relief as I headed out of the building. I kept stopping to look over my shoulder before boarding the school bus. Again I looked around for the unknown boy.

I stared out the bus's window as the school building grew distant. The bus driver called my name twice. "Your stop. Miss, wake up!" I hadn't felt or heard the screech of the bus's brakes when it came to a halt. The driver turned around to me and pointed toward the Bernards' house.

I walked slowly up the drive and opened the door. It was quiet inside. "Mrs. Bernard? Hello?" She wasn't around, but I heard Mr. Bernard's tractor out in the field.

Cautiously, I walked into the living room for the first time. My eyes skimmed the room, resting on the fireplace mantle. Making my way to the fireplace, I stepped up to the hearth. Tiptoeing to be at eye level with the mantle, I scanned the Bernards' framed family pictures. Stopping at one, I carefully picked it up. My heart skipped a beat. My knees jellied. Involuntarily my teeth chattered, and my body began to tremble. Gasping, I could feel my eyes rolling back in my head. Large hands lightly slapped my cheeks. Dazed with blurry vision, I struggled to focus.

"Girl! Girl?"

Mr. Bernard bent down and helped me up, retrieving the fallen picture beside me. I shuddered, and my lips quivered as I struggled for words. My shaky hands pointed to the picture he held. "I know him. That boy! I saw him. Him." I nodded and tapped the photo.

A cloud passed over his eyes and heavy sadness filled his voice. "This is my son, David." He rubbed his hand over the photo. "There'd been an accident in front of our house. It was David's birthday. Nine years old, only nine." He shook his head. "We'd bought him a blue bicycle. His favorite color. He was struck and instantly killed by a dairy truck." He lowered his head and wiped at his eyes.

Crying and now stuttering, I asked Mr. Bernard, "Did David stutter? I heard him stutter. At school. He did, Mr. Bernard!"

Looking suspicious and shocked, he cautiously answered, "Yes, David had speech problems."

"Mr. Bernard, David's not dead. He talked to me at school today. I saw him." I nodded, then shook my head. "Not dead. No!"

Mr. Bernard looked into my eyes. A grimace rippled across mappy lips, stretched — wobbled, then settled stiff in the corners of his mouth. "David is dead. Dead." He grabbed my arms and shook me. "Do you understand, Girl? Dead!"

My mouth flew open and I made a weak attempt to nod.

"Dead," he whispered.

Releasing me, he stood and turned his back. "Go to your room." He walked away. I let out a sob and ran to my bedroom. The rest of the day held uncomfortable silence, and it seemed that even Mrs. Bernard was unusually passive in her actions.

After supper and the cleaning of dishes, Mrs. Bernard sent us directly to bed. She gave no reason for the household's early retirement. I tossed and turned in my bed. Covers twisted and tangled, blending with my thoughts. Sleep finally took hold.

My nightmares were vivid. School lockers enclosed me. The small boy with hazel eyes was close to my face. He stuttered the word pretty over and over again, until it became lost in meaningless garble. I awoke drenched in a cold sweat, screaming.

Mrs. Bernard's abuse suddenly changed to indifference. She refused to look at me or speak to me.

"Mrs. Bernard, should I set the dinner table?" She grabbed the berry basket, walked right past me and out the back door.

After two weeks of uncontrollable nightmares, the Bernards called Mrs. Lindauer. Soon she came to get me. I climbed into her Bonneville, turned my gaze out the window, a retreat to silence. Letting my head fall back against the seat, I clenched my fists, squeezed my eyes to try to stop the tears that threatened.

"Your sisters will be happy to have you home," Mrs. Lindauer said in a soft voice.

I refused to look at her.

"Kim?"

She tried once more to engage conversation. "Why, Gayla has grown an inch at least." I nodded, biting at my lips, then turned back to the window, looked at the Bernards' house and silently wept the entire way back to the orphan asylum, while my birthday wish, and my forever family, faded in the distance of green farmlands.

I never spoke of David and the disturbing ethereal vision remained confined within my mind. I'd never know if I'd only imagined the little boy in the school hallway, but I'd always wonder how it was that I knew little David had stuttered.

As a grown woman, I'd reflect and wonder if the school incident and David was imagination or hallucination, brought on by stress, duress, or some type of post-traumatic syndrome of my own. More importantly, I'd come to realize that the dysfunction of the Bernard family lay with David's tragic death, and that his untimely death resulted in Mrs. Bernard's madness.

I accepted that some things in life could never, and maybe should never be explained.

Twenty-two
Hey lollee, lollee lo

I couldn't explain to Mother Superior why I didn't want to leave Saint Thomas, so I'd have to endure many more visits away from the orphanage. Some would be with prospective adoptive parents, others with random people looking to fill their own voids or smug self-gratifications. Sometimes, Gayla and I would go together. A weekend or a day trip was the norm.

These visits usually consisted of the family parading my sister and me in front of their friends, inviting shallow murmurs of sympathy, loud tsking noises and endless compliments regarding the generous benevolence of the family to take the little orphans in. My face would burn brightly with indignation and embarrassment. Gayla would give me a warning by gently elbowing me, thus preventing any outbursts.

Upon our return to Saint Thomas, the visiting family would grade the orphan's behavior. Using a long, typed checklist, the family made marks on manners, cleanliness, obedience, chores, etc. One bad mark from the visiting family would guarantee swift and severe punishment.

I spent many a day seated in the large foyer outside of Mother Superior's office, nervously swinging my legs back and forth on the old wooden bench, while the visiting family completed the evaluation. After the family left, Mother Superior would open her door.

An invitation into the office indicated punishment whereas a quick nod by Mother Superior meant I was excused. It ran fifty-fifty for me. Some families complained of my non-interaction and believed it demonstrated a lack of respect.

With many tears and much pleading, at age nine I started rebelling against the family visits away from Saint Thomas. I was terrified to leave the orphanage's familiarity, no matter how ruthless, to be thrust into the unknown. By stubbornly refusing, I was given harsh chores, ridiculed and beaten. Mother Superior eventually gave up on sending me to new families, restricting my visits to a single couple who seemed to enjoy my company, the Halls.

I peeled off the new pajamas the Halls had provided and looked indecisively at the matching shorts sets. Pink. Yellow.

Mrs. Hall, called, "Girls, breakfast will be ready in about fifteen minutes."

Before Gayla could lay claim, I grabbed the yellow set, dressed quickly and scurried out, banging the old camper's aluminum door along the way.

Inviting smells of woody pine mingled with campfire cooking and made my mouth water. I peered into the iron skillet. Thick jowl bacon and peppered eggs sizzled. Mrs. Hall popped a chunk of one of her homemade cinnamon rolls into my mouth. I smiled gratefully and she wrapped me in a tight hug. "Mr. Hall is over by the creek bed, scoot on over and practice your rock skipping before breakfast. You have time." I swallowed the sweet pastry dough, hugged her back and ran toward the creek.

Mr. Hall had no less than a dozen perfect skipping rocks beside his feet. He smiled, picked one up, rubbed it and handed it to me. I curled my index finger around the flat rock's edge, aimed low, brought my arm back past my waist and with a snap of my wrist, released. I watched the rock travel in a horizontal spin, skip three times across the placid waters. My jaw dropped. "Ohh."

Mr. Hall whispered, "My, my, Kim. Three perfect skips." Then he picked me up, spun me around counting three times until I was hoarse with laughter.

I watched as he did a perfect seven skip. I stood in awe for a moment, then grabbed his hands and we counted while we swung around seven times. Then he tousled my hair and we linked hands, each satisfied, and walked over to the campfire breakfast.

Later that evening Mrs. Hall walked Gayla and me over to the creek. "Cowgirl baths, girls," she smiled, handing us each our own sweet-smelling bar of soap. I took the soap, did a quick wash of face, feet and hands, dried off and scurried back to the evening campfire.

As usual, Mr. Hall started our badly orchestrated campfire singing concert, with the tree frogs generously lending tenor to our happy foursome.

"Oh, there was once a swagman camped in a billabong, under the shade of a coolabahs tree." Gayla, Mrs. Hall and I joined in, "Who'll come a-waltzing Matilda, with me?"

We had a brief interlude and ate toasted marshmallows. I looked at the Halls with contentment and smiled. "Mr. and Mrs. Hall, will you be adopting us soon?"

Then came a pregnant pause. The cricket song ceased until all I could hear were the soft gurgles of the nearby creek bed becoming louder, like a roaring waterfall in my head while I waited for their response. Finally Mrs. Hall answered, "Kim, Gayla, Mr. Hall and I want a baby. You understand?"

"Yes Ma'am," I said, excited. "I'll be the best big sister ever, I promise." I nudged Gayla, but she wasn't smiling. "Gayla, tell them how I take good care of Sister Charlotte's dog, Beigy, I'm a big girl, nine years old and I can be a big sister! Remember how I help you clean at your home, Mrs. Hall? I'll help you with the baby too, I promise, when you—"

"Kim. Kim, no, we want a ba—" Mrs. Hall started.

Mr. Hall cleared his throat. "We can talk about babies when you come for Thanksgiving this year. Let's sing, 'Hey Lollee.'"

"Hey Lollee, lollee, lo," Mr. Hall began.

Twenty-three
A picture is worth a thousand words

I looked out to the driveway, searching for my beloved Hall family. It was a few days till Thanksgiving, and the Halls hadn't called for me. I couldn't understand. They said they'd pick up Gayla and me for Thanksgiving and we'd talk about the baby.

I fought back the tears that choked. Discouragement and worry clouded my mind. All day was spent searching, waiting and running to the windows that exposed the circular drive in hopes that the Halls' brown Buick would magically appear.

Usually I only experienced this sadness on Sundays. This day was reserved for visitors of the orphans.

I remembered that once I'd received a rare and unexpected visit from my mother. With the visit came an infant. Diane had introduced him as my brother, Thomas. I was curious about this brother, but for the most part ignored him. My mother presented the small infant for me to hold, only to have me refuse. I was too afraid to handle the baby. But on Diane's next visit, she'd plopped him onto my lap and insisted that I hold him.

Given permission by Mother Superior to walk my mother out to her car, I shyly followed. We approached an old Cadillac. Seated on the passenger side was a small, pot-bellied man of half-Indian descent. He had a newspaper spread upon his lap with a tattered Brown & Williamson tobacco roller on top. A homemade cigarette dangled precariously out the side of his mouth as he fumbled to place a thin paper inside the roller. He looked up, grunted hello, then, taking pinches of Half and Half tobacco from a tin can, he sprinkled small amounts of it onto the tiny paper inside the roller and rolled himself a homemade cigarette.

Diane introduced Bryan as her husband. "An attorney, top of his class, with a promising career," she said. "Bryan fought courageously in World War II," she added.

But unknown to me at the time, he had been shipped home carrying the spirits of post-war demons. Eventually he fought these demons with his own weapon: alcohol.

Bryan's daily existence consisted of withdrawn silence, fisted bottles of alcohol and his beloved pouch of Half and Half tobacco.

Tragedy, I would think later. A non-existing life where his chief complaint was his endless grumbles about "those damn hippie potheads driving up the price of my cigarette papers."

On the surprise visit day at the orphanage, my mother eventually left with her husband and child, but not before she gave me a bag filled with crackers and a can of Cheese Whiz. I ran behind the building and greedily consumed most of the contents, almost making myself ill.

Today, I looked out the window expectantly, still awaiting the wonderful Hall family. Two days of constant watching had reduced me to tears, the stress proving too much.

The long stretch of a Saint Martin's summer had faded away, replaced by a sudden snap of wintry weather, indicating that the holidays were drawing near. A sob escaped as I rested my head against the cold pane of the window. I knew that a few of the lucky orphans would be going to distant relatives or a visiting family.

Thanksgiving was really no different than any other day for Saint Thomas's orphans. A special Thanksgiving Mass meant a longer Mass with the smothering incense. Chores were expected, and the day would end with some type of gristled meat, supposedly turkey.

I turned away from the window as I heard the loud whispers of my approaching friend. Jenny was flushed, excitement spilling out, and she motioned to me, wildly waving her hands.

"Come quick, Kimmi," she whispered breathlessly. "There are buses pulling in, and we're supposed to meet Sister Deloris Marie in the cafeteria. Hurry!"

I wiped my eyes, glanced out the window and sure enough, caught the tail end of a faded school bus heading toward the rear of the orphanage.

Jenny laughed, reached for my arm and pulled me forward. "Kimmi, let's go! Hurry!" She tugged my arm. "I've heard we're going somewhere. C'mon."

I freed my arm and peered once more out the window. I turned back to Jenny and smiled with anticipation and hopes that the forthcoming news would, indeed, be as Jenny said. I followed her down narrow, dark halls as we whispered about the puzzling report, trying to guess its meaning.

I sat beside my friend on the concrete floor of the cafeteria and listened to the huge nun who paced in front of us. Sister Deloris Marie's voice boomed off the cafeteria walls as she delivered the happy news. "You will be placed on buses and delivered to Fort Knox. Once there, you'll share a special Thanksgiving meal with the soldiers who reside there. Manners will be strictly enforced. Punishment for violations will be severe and swift." Sharply, Sister Deloris Marie reiterated her rules and her expectations.

With one last threatening sweep of the room, Sister Deloris Marie turned, her black robes whipping around her legs, and pointed toward the door, dismissing all of us to the waiting buses.

I sat happily beside Jenny and boasted, "I've been in a school bus before." I pointed to the window as the bus pulled away from the curb and, together, we managed to crack a window. The breeze was crisp and smelled wonderfully fresh as we giggled and breathed in as much as our lungs could hold.

We all buzzed infectiously with excitement and anticipation. Sister Camille, the young nun in charge of my bus, cocked a bushy brown brow, sending out frequent warning glances.

Whispered promises of snow threatened, and soon colored clouds spit large flakes, which twirled madly and landed sloppy wet on the bus windows. This induced more excitement and happy chatter.

Sister Camille turned to the back of the bus, glared and shot another warning glance. She turned back to address the bus driver and worried out loud about the weather.

The bus driver wasn't worried. "All's fine, Sister. I'll get you there safely." I wished for one hundred feet of snow so that we might never return to Saint Thomas.

Jenny and I delighted in fogging up the window, playing Tic Tac Toe, Hang Man, and drawing silly pictures. After tiring of that, Jenny took off her shoelace and tied each end together. Engrossed, we spent the remainder of the ride playing Cats 'n' Cradle. Our busy fingers looped the old dirty string around our tiny fingers, and quickly and efficiently transferred the string to the fingers of the other, with an artistic flair. A few hours later the bus ground to a halt.

The dull metal barracks looked intimidating. The driver had parked next to a giant concrete blob he called the Mess Hall, and Sister Camille began herding us off the bus, toward the hall.

I walked inside. The atmosphere was festive, filled with the hearty laughter of men. The soldiers stood in a greeting line. Dressed smartly, spit n' polished in their olive drab pickle suits and buffed black laced-up boots, they made an impressive picture.

The hosts were gracious greeting their orphaned guests. They handed out balloons, balls 'n' jacks, marbles, and playing cards. No child was forgotten. I smiled when one of the soldiers looped a colorful beaded necklace around my neck.

A tall, dark-haired soldier came toward Jenny and me. Smiling, he took one hand each and walked us over to one of the many long dining tables.

Metal tables had been transformed with white cloth, colorful balloons, and carved pumpkins. Delicious foods were plentiful, and the tables were bursting with large roasted turkeys, piles of freshly whipped potatoes, richly seasoned green beans, cranberries, and pies.

I nearly swooned with anticipation as the smells of the delicious foods tickled by nose. My stomach rumbled loudly and I wiped the unexpected drool from my mouth. It had been a long time since breakfast. We hadn't received lunch for the day, and it was already late afternoon.

Gesturing for us to be seated, the friendly soldier introduced himself. "My name's Bobby, I'm from McAllister, Oklahoma. Hello, little ladies!"

I smiled shyly.

Bobby pulled out a chair and seated himself between us. He entertained us with funny jokes, disappearing thumbs, disappearing noses, and magic tricks. Once, he made a quarter appear from behind my ear. And with a wink he gave it to me.

Chatter and laughter vibrated the Mess Hall. Glasses and silverware tinkled merrily. I'd never been so happy in my life or laughed so much! Politely sitting on my left hand, I watched as Bobby put a spoon upside down in his mouth. He made it wiggle up and down, making Jenny and me giggle until tears streamed down our cheeks.

I laughed so hard that I passed what seemed like a thunderous explosion of gas. Blushing furiously, I brought my hand up to my mouth, giggled, and looked around. I silently gave my dammit, and a thank goodness it was loud and not the silent ol' stinky type.

This only added to the hilarity. Taking advantage, Bobby blew fiercely on his arm to imitate the farting sound. The uproar of his hearty laughter blended with loud girlish squeals.

Bobby said, "You're stepping on frogs." I giggled and lifted both feet off the ground.

Putting the spoon back in his mouth, upside down, he wiggled it again. He handed me a spoon to do the same. I grinned and politely shook my head no.

He asked, "Do you want to be a big strong soldier?" Again Bobby encouraged me to try the spoon trick.

I smiled and shook my head, while Jenny piped in that, "She is too a big girl! She's nine. And Kimmi even cares for Sister Charlotte's dog!"

"Then big girls must be very smart. Are you smart enough to do the spoon trick?" The soldier challenged. "Eh?" His face was painted with mischief and merriment.

Again, Bobby put the spoon playfully in his mouth.

Handing me a spoon, he laughed. I looked at Jenny and grinned. I glanced around and saw a lone man standing in the corner with a large camera. The photographer waved, smiled at me, and turned to study the happy faces of the other orphans interacting with the soldiers.

Happily, and also wishing to please the soldier, I withdrew my left hand from under my bottom. Carefully, I placed the spoon as the soldier directed, upside down in my mouth. With the end sticking out, I wiggled it madly, up and down, while Bobby and Jenny laughed hysterically. It was an innocent act. Mere child's play mingled with cheerful mischief.

"Your green eyes are sparkling like diamond dust," Bobby said. I laughed and let the spoon dangle. Simultaneously, the photographer clicked his camera, capturing me being swept up in the innocence of the magically festive moment. I blinked from the photographer's flash, and my tablemates laughed.

After many thanks and many more hugs, we departed to board the buses. Quiet prattle and many yawns later, the motion of the bus lulled me into a peaceful, happy slumber.

As I slept, I was unaware of the fact that many would smile sweetly while glancing at the grinning little green-eyed orphan in their morning papers, while others would rage.

Upon our late arrival back to Saint Thomas, we stood single file inside the main foyer. Two large boxes sat to the right. We didn't have to be told to deposit all the gifts we received from the soldiers. We knew. Under the watchful eye of Mother Superior, one by one, we deposited the lovely colored beads, balls 'n' jacks, cards, and any other reminders of the special evening. The boxes would mysteriously disappear, never to be seen again. My only tangible reminder of the evening would be the forthcoming photograph.

The next morning I stood trembling, nervously clasping my hands. Mother Superior's tiny office seemed to be closing in on me. Staring down at the desk, I looked at the morning newspaper, which attested to my guilt. Taking up most of the page, my face stared back at me. The picture showed the dangling spoon hanging from my mouth, revealing my indiscreet table manners. A cold fear took hold, tears welled, and the mischievous grin on the print blurred in front of me as I fought to gain control.

Mother Superior picked up the paper, whipped it in the air, then smacked it down on her desk. I gasped, and the charming Kodak moment turned vile. She drummed the bony fingers of one hand on her desk while the other reached for a narrow fountain pen that she jabbed in my direction. "Explain!" She snapped.

My voice quaked, and my breath came in shallow gulps. "Mother, I . . . I'm sorry . . . The soldier . . ."

Mother Superior threw her pen down in disgust. "Go to Sister Deloris Marie this instant!"

For well over two weeks, I suffered the wrath and scorn of the nuns. Miraculously I survived the abuses; bloody nose, cut lips, swollen, popped blue-veined hands, withholding of food, and harsh verbal abuse, compliments of Sister Deloris Marie. It was the dispassionate stares and sudden shunning given by Sister Charlotte that would break my heart. She passed me in the hall three times and turned her head away on each. Usually she nodded and gave me a faint smile.

The merriment of the Thanksgiving dinner and my indecent table manners had cost me dearly. And because of my indiscreet table manners, I thought, I would forego my scheduled tonsillectomy surgery, which Mrs. Lindauer had prearranged for my sisters and me.

The nuns hid me when Mrs. Lindauer came to call. I watched tearfully from the three-story window of my dorm as my sisters rode off in Mrs. Lindauer's car to the city hospital. I moaned. "Stupid photograph." I didn't realize that my bruised and battered body had prevented my surgery, not the picture.

Why did I have to be so bad?

After many weeks of violence, I slowly regained my strength and acceptance back into the arms of Saint Thomas. Then came the delivery of copied photos, compliments of the newspaper. The final blow.

Sister Anthony's face grew red as she waved the black and white photo in front of me and the other children in my dorm. She shredded it furiously, leaving the fallen pieces to cascade down upon me. "Wild Injun!" She turned away.

I flinched. She looked back over her shoulder and sneered. "A picture is worth a thousand words."

And I cringed from the biting words and felt strange, outcast, like the wild, savage Injun the nuns always professed me to be.

Twenty-four
Purity

For a moment my groggy mind thought wild Injuns were attacking the orphanage. Cecilia Baker was kneeling on her bed screaming at the top of her lungs, drowning out the beating rain against the windows. Her eyes spilled out tears and awakened us all. Cecilia's panic rubberballed off the institution's dorm walls and invited a mad rush of alarmed orphans toward her bed.

There, in the middle of her bed, lay a huge fresh stain of bright red blood. The sight of such carnage induced hysteria in all of us. We were certain Cecilia was dying. Our piercing screams emulated Cecilia's.

This was the first time I'd seen blood appear without cause. I grabbed Jenny's arm and cried, "You can bleed without a beating, just from sleeping? Where is the blood coming from?" Jenny held on to me tight. "Ohh," and we screamed in unison.

Shielding her ears with clamped hands, Sister Anthony pushed her way through the crowd of screaming girls, her black robes flapping furiously behind her.

Panic, shrieks, and tears continued as Cecilia was dragged off her bed and down the hall. Her weeklong disappearance only added to the mystery, increasing everyone's confusion and fear.

Two weeks later, a strange woman came to call for the girls of Sister Anthony's dorm. Ushered into the lower bowels of Saint Thomas, we entered single-file into the basement of Sabrina Hall. The visitor greeted us impersonally and, in a no-nonsense voice, told us about the menstrual cycles of females. This was the first time in Saint Thomas's history that an outsider addressed this issue.

"Once a month you will bleed," she said. "Most of you will menstruate within a few years." Several large brown paper bags stood next to her podium.

I was only ten years old. I listened carefully, then I looked at Jenny, alarmed. "We'll bleed?" Jenny's jaw hung open. Small sobs escaped and eyes widened as our fears escalated.

The visitor creased her brow and raised her palm. "Silence." Reaching back into her brown bag, she pulled out a thick padded cloth and waved it in the air. She demonstrated its use by placing it inside the lining of a pair of panties, which she retrieved from another bag. Holding it up, she instructed us, "Place the padded cloth in your panties when you begin to bleed." She then handed each of us several pads. "You can place these in your lockers for future use. Furthermore, I expect purity from each and every one of you!"

Reaching into a different bag, she pulled out white cotton gloves and instructed us in their use. "These are to be worn during bath and bedtime, so no impure touches or thoughts dirty you."

I looked down at my red, cracked hands, already trying to figure out how I'd use the gloves for protection during floor scrubbing.

Last of all, she talked briefly about sexual intercourse. "Marriage comes from the loving hand of God. This sacrament is called Holy Matrimony, and draws the man and woman together in sacred union to produce children."

She ignored the several hands that rose up to question, saying simply, "God commands us to multiply, and we must be faithful to Him."

That was the end of discussion from the mysterious visitor. No questions were allowed or deemed necessary.

Leaving Sabrina Hall in a single file, we paused to receive our new white gloves, along with a final admonishment, "Never bathe or sleep without them."

This added to our uncertainty and did nothing to abate our fears. Mornings were spent carefully combing our bedcovers, looking for the telltale signs of the ominous menstrual cycle.

Later in the week, Sister Anthony carried bags into the dorm. With them came a new curiosity. The nun peeked inside, then, repulsed, emptied all three bags onto the dormitory floor. I was astonished to see colorful flowered clothing. They were long breeches! Men's breeches!

Bemused, I took my pair alongside the other girls. I rubbed the soft homespun cotton pants and marveled at the pretty yellow-petaled flowers.

"Thank you, Sister," we all chimed in. Sister Anthony only snarled.

Another bag contained full-length white cotton slips. Sister Anthony ordered, "Slips must be worn from now on, underneath the breeches and all clothing." Stomping away as quickly as she had come, Sister Anthony left no time for questions.

Jenny and I giggled nervously as we prepared to try on our man breeches over the new full-length slips. Instructions for their use were not included. More giggles emerged, as Jenny put both legs into one leg of the breeches. Unsuccessful attempts made us topple over more than once. Trying to get both legs inside the breeches' legs, with the full-length slip tucked in, was no easy task.

We finally collapsed on the floor in mad, muffled laughter. When at last we'd accomplished our painfully simple task, we looked to each other for affirmation. Jenny laughed and pointed to my yellow flowered breeches. I looked down and wrinkled my nose. It felt as if I was wearing a diaper, and it most certainly looked like it. I studied Jenny and glanced around, relieved to see that I wasn't the only one with the diaper effect. The hidden slip was obvious, as it ballooned the breeches outward.

"This has to be the silliest thing ever to happen here, wearing man breeches!" whispered Jenny.

I smiled and nodded in agreement and again marveled at the yellow flowers. "But they sure are pretty."

"Mmm, they are," Jenny agreed.

In the back of my mind the secret visitor's words and cloth pads nagged at me. The pads remained hidden in my locker, tucked within the folds of my clothes. No one else in Sister Anthony's dorm ever bled, but I'd heard the older girls in Sister Martin's dorm were starting to bleed.

I studied this. For some odd reason this brought me a small comfort. I felt the links of my chains were somehow weakening because of the mystery blood. I could almost taste the promises of distant, mysterious freedoms, and I smiled.

We never knew that the maturing and changing of our bodies, a girl's natural rite of passage, were being ignored and suppressed, or that the man breeches were a hushed solution to still the fears of the nuns, to augment, and keep control.

Twenty-five
A chat with Satan

2006

It was late in the afternoon in July 2006 when I received the urgent, unexpected phone call. Surprised, I listened to my attorney's assistant explain. "A legal mediation between the nuns' organization and the former orphans will take place tomorrow."

Two years had passed, and now the Sisters of Charity wished to settle the lawsuit. It had been well over a year since the exhausting deposition. And it didn't sound too promising.

The same legal assistant called back a few days later. "The Sisters of Charity have presented an offer. You, as well as the others, need to consent to it. It's a settlement offer that all forty-five must agree on. Would you give your consent to this amount?"

"Another slap," I murmured.

An insulting settlement amount. It was not enough to compensate robbed childhoods. But then again, what amount could?

"Withholding the food again," I mumbled to no one in particular." Likely, it was the best William could do," I admitted. All avenues had been exhausted, and what with the statute of limitations working against us, it was really all we could expect.

"It looks bleak," the assistant said.

"Yes, thank you," I told him. I hung up, only to receive yet another call the next day informing me that the nuns had raised the settlement offer. How very clever, I thought, applauding the proficient intent behind the meaning. What better way to get everyone on the same page?

"Whatever William feels is best." I agreed. "Time to move forward." *Too many years looking in the rearview.*

The archdiocese of Louisville, Kentucky had long since been released from the lawsuit due to the sticky statute of limitations laws. It struck me that the Church had abandoned the Sisters of Charity and now used her as a shield and a diversion.

The assistant rambled on. "It would also send a strong message to the world, showing the injustices inflicted by the Church and by the nuns' organization. With it would come restoration of dignity, and more importantly, closure for you and the others."

"What the—?" *Dignity in exposing humiliations is more like it.* It felt as if I'd stood naked in front of a crowd, and it disgusted me. I would have to die a thousand deaths to restore that part. Dignity as in pride? I put the phone back in its cradle and paced across the hardwoods of my bedroom while rubbing my throbbing temples.

Closure, he had said. *Closure?* Now that's a word open for discussion. If only those parts of my mind could close.

I wouldn't lose it. I never lost it. I was strong.

"I am." I blinked back a tear. "Strong," I whispered.

I was becoming quietly hysterical, if that were possible. *Quiet hysteria.* I laughed and had a maniacal thought; I want my tears back, my voice. Then I felt the darkness of closure, and I struggled against it. My world cried no, my feelings bled raw, and my mind screamed in protest.

"Who wore the face of GOD?" I startled my sleeping cat, and she mewed loudly in protest. The dog barked, the phone rang, and everyday household noises faded, until I could no longer hear anything but the screams of my own once-silent voice.

Who? Who wears the face? 'Whoever causes one of these little ones who believe in me to sin, it would be better for him if a great millstone were put around his neck and he were thrown into the sea.' Anybody listening to the Good Book? Anybody? Who was reading Matthew, Mark and Luke?

He who had worn the face of God hid behind God's face to mask his evil deeds. Who wore the face of God? Certainly not the twisted demons who robbed.

For only the *innocent child* could wear the face of God.

I let out a sob. My hands shook. I fought against losing it as I cradled my head in my hands and shook my head in denial. I slid down the bedroom wall, hugged my knees to my chest, and rested my chin on them. I was five years old again. My hair hung, shielded my face and hid my tear-stained cheeks from my riotous soul. I felt so small, like I was melting into the drywall. My voice grew tiny and my no's faded.

Then I surrendered the innocent heart of my childhood and extended my hand to Satan. I walked into Hell, conversed with demons past, found my stolen tears and painfully wept, tasting those acrid drops. Shaking my fists to the heavens, I questioned my God many times, "I'm so disappointed in you, God. So disappointed," I sobbed. "You," I fought to catch my breath, "you forgot to tell the world I was supposed to be a princess, God, a princess! Somebody's princess. So disappointed, so very . . ." Until I fell asleep on my stomach, as usual. Because like most abused kids, I had always slept face down and carried this habit into adulthood. I would continue to do so for protection. When I awoke, more tears rained down. I cried for my childhood, which was lost to me, and for all those who had worn the face of God, still lost.

Exhausted, I got up to wash off my tears. I looked into the mirror and decided. It wouldn't do for my family to see me like this, so I took a cool cloth, wiped away the past, looked into my heart and decided I didn't want to go there again, or stay there, for that matter.

I'd found my stolen tears, my voice, in my family, my life.

"I refuse to spend a moment more of my life jaded by this," and I vowed: "I will not be broken. I'm unbreakable. Strong by God's grace."

I finally came back in from the cold, rain-drenched streets of my mind and stepped up to the warm hearth God had provided me: my family — my *forever* family.

Twenty-six
Irony

2006

The rain had stopped, and I gave a smile to the waiter as he directed us to the outdoor patio and seated me in our favorite spot. I settled comfortably in the chair and absorbed the eclectic Highlands area of Louisville, Kentucky. The overhead Havana fans quickly cooled, bringing relief from the sticky August evening. I pointed to the beautiful velvet-blue skies, streaked with iris and reds, "Look, Joe, God painted the sky. Wow, it's stunning tonight."

He looked at me. "Indeed, I can see He created a masterpiece."

After all these years, Joe could still make me blush.

The waiter arrived with my favorite drink, sweet tea.

"Is there a day goes by when you don't have tea? Even the waiter has you pegged," Joe teased.

I laughed. "I hear they're using tannin to make tea soap now."

"I think you've already been baptized in it."

I raised a glass in toast. "To the South's holy water." I took a sip, relaxed, and watched the passersby.

The Bardstown Road area of the Highlands was our favorite place to dine and kick back. Brimming with unique shops and diverse restaurants, its alluring atmosphere delighted us. The old neighborhood was a charming melting pot of colorful characters, talented artists, and interesting businesses. Joe and I grinned as we watched two purplish-orange-haired boys pass, their skateboards dangling at their sides. Across the narrow street, old man Espositi placed a generously-filled bowl of homemade gelato in front of a laughing couple seated on his patio.

"Joe . . ."

He smiled and reached for the menu. "We'll grab a quart to take home." He pretended to study the menu. "I'll serve you in bed."

"Mmm." I raised an approving brow and reached for my menu. Joe put his down, caught my hand and held it. His whiskey-brown eyes spoke what his voice didn't. He put his free hand up to his pendant.

"Make a wish," I whispered. "The clasp has fallen in front." I reached up, straightened it and traced my finger over the inscription. *I love you like salt loves meat.*

My eyes met his. He pulled me close and savored my features with his gaze. Then he gave me a warm, tender kiss. Heat flushed our faces, and we parted and rested our foreheads together.

My hairdresser walked past, rapped the table, smiled and continued on. We both looked up and grinned a little. I picked up the menu. "Ahem, shall we order then? The sooner we eat, the sooner we can get home."

With all said and done, Kentucky was home. No matter how far I strayed, whether for business or pleasure, I always looked forward to coming back. With the beautiful changing seasons, the unpredictable stick-around-a-minute-it'll-change weather, and the majestic bluegrass horse farms, I couldn't imagine living anywhere else.

My cell phone interrupted my peaceful thoughts. "It's final, the mediation was successful, and the lawsuit is legally finished," William's secretary stated. "Could you come in and sign the papers and pick up your settlement check?"

I entered William McMurry's office a few days later. Arriving twenty minutes before my appointment time of nine o'clock, I was surprised to find a few people already milling around. Forcing a bright smile while murmuring polite good mornings, I glanced at the people. The faces were unfamiliar. I quickly bypassed them and made my way to the receptionist's desk.

I had hoped to avoid meeting any of the former orphans by arriving before my scheduled time. Maybe the other people had the same thought. As far as meeting the former orphans, it was just too painful to see the haunting past reflected in their eyes, the histories that shadowed their future. I did not wish to recreate this painful past with random, superfluous chatter.

On rare occasions, my sisters and I would speak of our childhood home. Even then it was only among us. Such conversations were always hushed, vague, and brief, then tucked away like an old worn picture in a broken frame.

The settlement monies would change some lives. As I looked to the former orphans, I thought about my own sister, Gayla, and predicted that the money would be a detriment to her, inducing idiocy and bringing with it ill-fated serendipity. She would probably use it for drugs, and I worried about more harm it would bring her.

I sighed as I remembered it had been over twenty years since I last saw her. Gayla had chosen Diane's path, and I had subsequently warned her to steer clear of mine. As an adult, I had choice, and I was determined that my life would no longer be controlled or influenced by those who abused drugs and or alcohol. For this, I harbored no guilt.

I'd left the offer of sisterhood open should Gayla ever change paths. It had broken my heart to part ways, but Gayla continued to follow our mother's addicted path, turning her back on me.

My sweet sister Caity? I'd found out days before the litigation ended that Caity had dropped out of the lawsuit many months before. She hadn't told me. I'd given my sister the blues while she danced around the subject, annoying me and causing me to lose patience. Caity finally broke down and, many tears later, told me why she had dropped out of the lawsuit.

"I can't deal with all this," she said over the phone.

"Caity, it's an emotional process for all."

"It's just too much stress for me," she whispered.

"You're not making sense." I frowned. "There's more. What is it that you're keeping from me?"

"Have you ever thought, God will punish us if we punish the Catholic Church and their priest and brides of Christ? Maybe I'd get the cancer back."

"What?" My hand tightened around the phone. "Put aside the Catholic Church's brainwashing for once and listen to yourself. Look at all you've suffered because of the RCC's clergy. You're being foolish, Caity, you're—Oh, this is crazy. Fix it!"

"It's too late." Her voice cracked. "I signed legal papers, releasing me."

"No," I moaned. "It's okay, Cat." I clenched my teeth and released my white-knuckled grip of the phone, "Lil' sis will make it right."

And I would. Promises made, promises kept.

The secretary led me out of the waiting area and into William's office. William rose from his desk and shook my hand. I used my free hand to offer him a file. I remained standing while he settled back into his chair.

"This is for you, William," I explained, "and congratulations as well."

I'd written a childish outline of my life at the orphanage, my inept attempts at word slinging. But the gift came from the heart, and though its value may have been negligible to many, it was priceless to me and, I hoped, to him as well. It was uncomfortable, but somehow necessary.

This man needed to know that all his efforts were not measurable solely by the size of a settlement check. Perhaps for his children as well, so they would know their daddy had walked courageously and at times alone, where others had dared not tread. I'd decided long ago, when the legal proceedings began, no matter the outcome, to end it with this, opening old wounds, pouring blood and tears into pages, creating lexis, to gift William with my silent words that now screamed out loud. He'd always know and never forget that he gave back stolen tears and voice, to the ones without families: the orphans.

The TV news had quoted William, stating, "The settlement marked the first time in United States history any victims of a Catholic orphanage had recovered payment due to past abuses." The morning's newspaper announced the settlement, and the Sisters of Charity publicly proclaimed their innocence, while privately conceding. Then they sent out secret individual invitations to make nice, an offer to chat. Thus a lame apology letter from the nuns to the orphans was enclosed with each settlement check.

Sides were taken. Those who were blinkered and in denial of the Catholic Church's clergy abuse scandal fueled the public news media, screamed virtuously and sensationalized the legal decision for diversion and debate, stultifying its intent due to ignorance and lack of facts. Nonetheless, I believed our main goal had been accomplished. Justice, such as it was, had been served. But I predicted that more truth would come to light about this powerhouse, the Roman Catholic Church.

I looked down at William's desk and saw scattered paperwork that indicated busy work, then I looked back up at him thoughtfully.

"Thank you, Kim." He stood. "I look forward to reading it." His smile was appreciative.

I stepped back. For a fleeting second, our gazes merged, and I glimpsed into the man's soul before he could shield it. Surprised, I turned my head and gave an inward gasp. I was saddened by the truth, as it was heart-telling. His eyes revealed his emotions, the pain and the losses he had suffered due to his quest for others, and I suspected those losses far outweighed any material gains.

Heart-telling because a man couldn't give so much without sacrificing, I knew.

There would be many who would never fully understand or care about the sacrifices he had endured, but I, at that moment realized it had taken its toll on him, his family, friends, and associates. All that couldn't be masked by a smile and gracious handshake.

I found out later that William had indeed lost almost everything, including his family and home, because of his pursuit of justice for others, others who had suffered from the injustices of the Roman Catholic Church's clergy. Just the thought of dealing with forty-five people, carrying so much fragile and emotionally scarred baggage, would have been enough to send a saint running toward the gates of Hell.

I'd walked into his life, giving him my battered childish heart, expecting miracles, demanding. Others had followed and would continue after me. Never in my life had I imagined anyone coming forward to champion for justice and successfully bring to light the past abuse of the orphans. And for this I was immensely grateful. It humbled me that this man would walk with me.

William *knew* who wore the face of God.

I looked at the large wall of pictures behind William and studied a framed glossy, which showed him skydiving. I grinned. Adrenaline junkie? Stress reliever? It would take him a lot of jumps to eradicate the stresses of this case.

I looked at William. "How do you cope? All this . . ." I glanced down at the huge stack of papers. "How does *William* cope? Deal with the anger?"

"It's important to remember that you cannot be angry and smart at the same time." He paused. "I prefer to stay smart." He gave a small smile, shoved his hands deep into his pockets and glanced down. "But, I don't always cope," he said softly. He cocked his head and looked at me. "It is often not pretty ..."

I nodded, knowing he raged against everyone who stood in his way of justice for these victims. And that he'd dedicated his life to all victims, not just to clergy abuse victims.

"And, I guess I want a better world for my kids, and I want companies and people in positions of power to be held accountable."

I signed the final paperwork. William handed me a check and some copied papers, then he shook my hand. Looking at William, unable to completely suppress my grin, I said, "You know William, this money will have to go back to the Catholics."

His expression transformed from friendliness to disbelief and finally to a slow burn. Steel eyes cooled and threatened to tantrum. *"What?"*

Holding up my hand, I explained. "Tuition," I stated matter-of-factly.

William looked blank for a moment then slowly grinned. He had forgotten that my child attended Catholic high school.

"In fact, William, the settlement amount is almost to the exact penny needed to pay the remaining years of my child's Catholic tuition. Irony or what?" I smiled.

He laughed. "Irony indeed."

Twenty-seven

Home \ hom\ n:

the social unit formed by a family living together

Like most kids I wasn't entirely sure of a lot of things. I was almost sure Sister Deloris Marie was going straight to Hell. I was pretty sure Sister Charlie was already there. I wasn't quite sure whether I'd follow or not. But there were two things I was sure of. I'd been living in Hell on earth with dead Sister Charlie for years. And today I was walking out of Hell.

Sister Deloris Marie rapped the top of my head with her knuckles. "Eat your breakfast, Missy. Even ungrateful girls should know better than to waste food." She peered down over her spectacles and gave another hard crack to my head. "It's bad, and bad girls go to Hell."

I stared at the greenish-gray bowl of runny oatmeal, then tried my hardest not to gag. In the end my hardest wasn't good enough. I sneaked over to the trash can and almost had my bowl scraped clean when the nun came up behind me, yanked my hair back and struck me hard across the face with her metal spoon.

It hurt, but not like usual, because I knew it would be the last morning she'd hurt me. The last morning I'd have to eat Satan's favorite food. And the last morning I'd leave the table hungrier than when I sat down.

At ten o'clock this morning my mother was taking me away from the orphan asylum.

I stood in the orphanage's large entry foyer with my sisters and prodded my bloody, tender nose. Any minute now, Mother Superior would give the nod to my sisters and me to file out of the institution. My stomach contracted, betraying my mixed emotions of fear and hope. I clutched my belly.

Then, Mother Superior gave the signal, and on a perfect sunny day in June, 1967, we walked out of the old asylum for the last time. And on that picture perfect sunny day of my final departure, I left with nothing more than the clothes on my back, my treasured scarab bracelet, and a small unexpected hug from Sister Charlotte. A hug abruptly given and just as abruptly withdrawn, leaving behind only a whispered scratch from the old nun's wool headdress brushing against my tear-stained cheek. It would be the solitary balm given for years of brutal abuses delivered.

In single file we made our way out to the circular drive. Mother Superior shut the door quietly behind us. I stopped and looked over at the silent playground, running along the narrow stretch of dirt road, and wondered if Jenny and Byrdie would finish their work in time to see me off.

Beyond, I could see those rolling, rolling, and more rolling hills of Kentucky. The hills that had captured so many tears. I'd spent so many years dreaming of what lay beyond, watching the sun set on those hills, changing them from bluegrass green to greenish black.

Byrdie Maize ran around the corner of the building, her threadbare oversize dress flapping in the wind. "Wait!" she hollered, waving her arms and running up to me. "I just got done scrubbing Sister Deloris Marie's floors. Whew! I thought she'd never let me out." She bent over, rested her hands above her knees to catch her breath. "She wouldn't let Jenny leave until she finished her floor scrubbing."

I glanced down at Byrdie's cracked and bloody knees, looked back up and saw Byrdie lick a trail of blood off her freshly busted lip. Her naturally dark-brown cheek was darker from a new bruise.

"Here, Kimmi, a present." She lifted a string of clover hanging from around her neck and handed it to me.

I pushed the necklace carefully down over my head and adjusted it on my neck and smiled. "Thanks, Byrdie. I'll miss you." I gave her a hug.

"It's okay, Kimmi. This weekend, my daddy is coming from California to get me. This weekend, didn't I tell you?"

I winced. Over the years there'd been a lot of *this weekends* for Byrdie.

Pamela tugged on my sleeve. "C'mon, we're waiting."

I gave a small wave. "Bye, Byrdie."

"I'll come and visit you when Daddy picks me up this weekend." She waved back, then turned abruptly when one of the nuns poked her head out of the building and yelled for her.

My sisters piled into the back seat of our mother's old Cadillac. Pamela pulled me in and gave me the window seat. Diane, my absentee mother for life, lit a cigarette, reached over the cracked leather bench seat and grasped my hand. I felt its twitch and smelled the alcohol and tobacco waft, then wrap around her sluggish speech. "My ba–bay–bee?"

Uncomfortable, I withdrew my hand from hers and peered out the window at my childhood home. Mother Superior stood behind the tall pane of her office window, hands linked, waiting. Watching.

I rubbed the clover's nut-brown blossoms across my lips. Back and forth. Back and forth.

I wondered why Mother Superior was letting me go after all these years, why she was sending me away with this woman who felt so wrong. A new punishment? Like the time she sent me off to stay with the violent, foster farm family. I wondered why she didn't just have my head dunked in the toilet or have me force-fed like she'd done so many times before. Or just have Sister Charlotte give me more drugs, her never-fail way to keep all of us orphans in line.

What had changed? The questions whirled in my mind, but none as loud as, *why hadn't Mother Superior found me an adoptive family, my forever family, like the one I'd been praying for all these years.*

I chewed on my bottom lip. I'd been bad. You go to Hell when you're bad. Maybe I hadn't prayed enough. You go to Hell for not praying.

Then Diane leaned toward me and offered me a welcome-home gift: a sample of Avon's Pinky Dink Pink lipstick. I hesitated. The cigarette dangled from her red lips, an inchworm ash grew long and hung suspended near my arm. Then she wagged the lipstick tube and the inchworm landed on my wrist. I felt its bite, brushed it quickly away and shrank back against Pamela. Diane took no notice.

"Go ahead, Kimmi." Gayla nudged me. "We're not orphans anymore. Right, Mom?"

Diane managed a ghost of a smile then nodded.

I smiled shyly in return, shook my head and left the offer dangling. Gayla gave a disgusted grunt, reached over and took the lipstick from Diane. With an air of smug defiance, she painted her lips, then slapped the lipstick into my palm.

Diane whined. "It's obvious *Kim Michele* doesn't want her present."

"As—" I stopped, then swallowed my words when I realized I'd almost quoted Sister Charlotte's favorite saying: *As obvious as God's buzz on a bee.*

I twisted the bottom of the tube, looked into my mother's eyes and watched them slowly blink once. Pamela elbowed me and cut me a warning glance. "Just do it. Don't make her angry."

I drew a pink line across my palm, studied the intense color, then narrowed my eyes.

Caity patted my shoulder. "C'mon, try it."

I brought the lipstick slowly up to my mouth, looked over to Mother Superior's window and met her gaze. "No Pinky Dink Pink for you, Mother Superior," I whispered.

My big sisters giggled. And like putting lipstick on a pig, I smeared a thick coat across my lip. It felt soft. Good.

I grinned, then kept smearing, pressing harder to coat and cloak and erase the orphan in me.

Twenty-eight
No hearts but the broken

1982

I returned to Saint Thomas-Saint Vincent Orphan Asylum years later as a young woman. My insistent sister, Caity, dragged me back. I was too overwhelmed to reply when she said, "We'll go back to the orphanage together. I want to try and retrieve any childhood records, before it closes and gets demolished. The obscene place is finally being torn down to make room for an elite subdivision. We'll stay just long enough to get the records, I promise. Not a second longer. Now quit being a baby."

The road twisted narrowly through country meadows. I sat quiet in the passenger seat while Caity drove to our childhood home. I looked over at my sister, hesitated and struggled for words while a flood of dark emotions ran through me.

"Cat?"

"Hmm?"

"Do you remember the holy cards?"

"Sure. Why?" She gave me a glance.

"I was just wondering. Did you ever receive the holy card of Saint Dymphna?"

Caity frowned and redirected her attention to the road.

No "aha" moment there, I decided, or either she was scanning her memory banks of times she'd probably flushed away long ago, for a memory that didn't wreak pain. I turned my gaze back to the passing countryside and fidgeted with my broken pinky finger, the badge earned from the nuns' over-corrections. The words slipped out of my head before I could marshal them back. "Hmm, I wonder if you can even be Catholic without broken pinky fingers?" I sighed, then tucked my hands under my bottom to still, them and myself, like we'd been taught.

Caity released a hand from the steering wheel and inspected her fingers. "Nope."

As we approached the weather-beaten statue of the Blessed Virgin Mary, a knot formed in my stomach and my bones felt as if they had frosted over. I clutched my throat to chase away the choking panic sensation.

"Hey, look, the statue's still here," Caity's eyes were glued to the pitted concrete figure.

"Yes," I barely whispered. I looked over to the Blessed Virgin Mary, seated in the middle of the massive circular drive. With compassionate arms extended, she welcomed us. An unintentional irony: the woman held up by the Church as the model for all women, the woman who nurtured the Son of God, giving an implied blessing to past horrors inside. Before those thoughts could lead me down the path I'd worked so hard never to revisit, I looked around for people or passing cars . . . anything to distract myself from where I was at the moment and the thoughts that might just rip my mind apart for good.

Caity merged into the drive and parked. For a second our eyes met, then she sighed and pulled up the emergency brake. My hands trembled as I reached for the door handle. Pulling back the latch, I pushed open the door and put one foot out on concrete then looked back at Caity. Feeling much like a trapped animal quivering outside the hunter's shack, I frowned at her, then moved my other foot out of the car and smacked it hard on concrete.

We slammed the car doors shut in unison and I whispered, "I can't believe we came back. And even more so, I can't believe I let you talk me into coming back."

Caity smiled at me to defuse an argument. I was surprised to find the orphan asylum looked the same as the day I'd left. Even though I was a grown woman, the old building still looked gloomy and huge as it loomed over me. It should look smaller, and I'd expected it to, as logic would assume when one faces a structure from childhood. But it looked the same, just as it did in my nightmares; full of shadows and secrets.

I shivered. I was quite sure if I touched the old bricks, they'd turn rhythmic, beat slowly, breathe silent, until its deep inhalation consumed, holding me in an eternal prison like when I was little. Hugging myself, I tried to still my shaking. Caity's pleas to enter the front door bounced off me, and my green eyes narrowed when she pushed. "No way!" I hissed. "Stop!"

Knowing my temper, she finally relented and walked toward the building alone, calling back over her shoulder. "Send the cavalry if I don't come back." I couldn't tell if she was full of forged bravado in order to literally face old demons, or if she was reentering the orphanage again as an adult to save her own life and sanity. Whatever her mission, and as much as it hurt me to be unable to join her in that moment, I just couldn't. Maybe if I prayed for herculean strength, I thought, and did just that with a quick volley of "O help me, sweet baby Jesus."

My eyes softened and I tossed her a lopsided grin. "Will one Wild Injun do?" I asked, not knowing how my spirit had become infused with such lightness in this darkest moment. And our sister hearts laughed, knowing.

As she disappeared inside, I realized I'd been holding my breath. I released it and inhaled deeply. The early summer air smelled of wild locust blossoms and fresh grasses mixed with sweet honeysuckles. Turning my gaze west, I scanned the playground, and a childish thought occurred to me. I wondered as to the whereabouts of the tiny paper scraps on which I'd written my pleas for help, then randomly buried. I'd buried so many things here. My birthday bracelet so the nuns wouldn't find it. How many times had I buried and reburied the scarab bracelet, I wondered. How often had I buried deep within myself the horrors of my youngest years?

The country air suddenly turned pungent. Breezes kicked up and hummed hidden secrets, enveloping the old asylum, soiling pure country airs. I wrapped myself in a tight hug and looked toward the entrance grounds. I was surprised to see they were still being manicured.

In the distance, the vast meadows were painted generously with summer wildflowers. Beyond that were the bountiful fruit orchards where I'd spent many a day picking apples, peaches and pears. *Fruit for the nuns and priest to feast upon.*

For a moment a ghoulish scene of rotted apple fields in the Garden of Eden flashed across my mind. I forced it away by concentrating on the dirt country road lined with lush cherry trees standing in front of the dense woods, with the distant promise of wildlife.

Across the way, beside the now voiceless playground, stood the faded groundskeepers' cottage. The picket fence had all but fallen, leaving only a few lonely wooden planks. The McCrearys' once meticulous gardens were all but gone, filled with tall wild onions and scraggly pokeweeds, holding no vestige of Mrs. McCreary's gifted green thumb. The quaint old dairy barn and steel grain silo stood peacefully to the left. The cows were long gone in preparation for its demolition. The old brick smoke stack still stood and, in the end, it would take two tries and eleven sticks of dynamite to bring it down.

I stood and let whispers of memories sheath me. Closing my eyes against the bright sunshine, I willed calm to chase and erase the haunting memories and the gooseflesh from my arms.

The main entry's ill-fitted door rattled as Caity pushed it open and walked out. She was empty-handed, defeated, and silenced. I had neither words nor the heart to chide her for her foolishness.

Do demons have hearts, I wondered? There were no hearts but the broken at Saint Thomas.

The drive home was silent.

Twenty-nine
Eternity's Kiss

Father Lammers died the year I turned twenty-six. Time killed him, or so I imagined. Whether it was the time he spent thinking about what he'd done to all those children that ate at him, or the time I'd spent thinking of the very same thing. I wasn't quite sure.

I remembered once, when I was just seven years old, Father Lammers summoned me to his private quarters. He gave me wine and I'd gagged and choked on its taste. I'd wanted to scream but my little voice couldn't. He'd unzipped his pants and I'd been too frightened to move.

I sat at the kitchen table, sipped my coffee and stared at the small print of the obituary section. Through the aromas of coffee beans and newsprint, I smelled long-ago tobacco smoke, the medicinal tang of Brylcreem and evil. His evil.

I wondered if God would turn him into a new Prometheus for using us orphans as his playthings. I wondered if the Devil had a special room prepared for him with big strong assistant-devils who would bind him to a stake and send down a flock of turkey buzzards to feed upon his privates every minute of eternity.

For three days I walked into my kitchen and sat down at the table and re-read Father Lammers's obituary. And for several hours on each of those days, I thought about eternity. His and mine.

Not a bad eternity, I thought as I reached for the box of Cocoa Puffs and grinned at the cartoon bird cuckooing his morning cheer. I topped off my son's cereal bowl. My son beamed up at me with a chocolate-kissed mouth. *Not bad at all.*

Thirty
Mother's final secret

1998

I picked up an empty chocolate candy bar wrapper off the ash-burned carpet and sat it on the cluttered glass coffee table.

Sitting in silence, hands trembling, I awaited my sister's arrival. My mother's small, dingy apartment was depressing. A thick pall of death and stale smoke kissed and lingered in the airless room, reminding me of long ago Benedictions, and I could taste its bile. I fought for release as the coroner left quietly with my mother's body.

As expected, years of drug and alcohol abuse had finally taken their toll. Waiting for my sister, I thought about the countless ways in which my mother and her children had been ravaged by her seeking solace in substances. How I'd hurdled the temptation to be victimized again like others I'd known who had been sucked down the tubes of alcohol and drug addiction.

I wanted to pray, but my mind was churning way too fast to turn to a quick-prayer-for-strength. Or maybe my heart just wasn't ready to speak the words, "forgive us our trespasses as we forgive those who trespass against us . . ."

I was relieved when Caity arrived within the hour. She walked up to me but stopped, as if not sure whether to come closer or leave. Then she perched beside me on the edge of our mother's faded couch and handed me a legal document. "I think you should have this." She shrugged and looked away.

My mother, Diane, the forever drama queen, would not go to her grave in silence. She would leave behind a special parting gift for me – a shocking revelation contained in a cold official document.

"Where did you get this?"

Caity stood up and averted her eyes from mine by absent-mindedly brushing the cat and dog hairs from her pants.

"Caity?"

"We need to start cleaning up here," she said, walking toward the hall.

Bitterness overshadowed my solemnity as I absorbed the powerful words on the faded page. I let the tears fall. The document confirmed my past suspicions and would eventually lead to the true identity of my natural father; a prominent physician in the community.

I didn't share the same father as my siblings? I clutched the paper in my fist, wishing I could crush the facts of my past as easily. It was true; I bore little resemblance to my older sisters, physically, mentally, or emotionally.

Bitter thoughts reared up in my head. Had my father known about me and acknowledged my existence, my life's path would not have led me into the orphan asylum. *Had my father known me . . . does my father know me . . . does my Father know me . . .* invaded my thoughts, like a continuous looping chant gone whacko like a cheap dime-store bouncy-ball.

I have no idea how long I sat slumped on that filthy couch, grasping the paper, until I realized I was standing and struggling to take in a deep breath. I looked down, amazed to see my hands folded in prayer and was hit by an unexplained tingling charge that strengthened and energized me.

My mind screamed with a resolute power. *The orphanage didn't break me, and I'm sure not going to let this blindside hit break me either. I'm my own, strong woman, and I've carved a good life for myself out of the muck and rubble and crap I was given to work with!* I smoothed out the wrinkled paper, folded it neatly and tucked it in my purse – tucked the knowledge away, merging it with the other memories, out of sight, in that small shoebox on my uppermost mental shelf. I would turn my soul and blend into its tight curve. No yield necessary.

Eventually, I would find the strength and benefit of praying for Diane's soul. I wanted my mother to find peace as much as I wanted to lay to rest her many self-destructive demons who had been her constant companions. Burying them along with her would give me gratitude and forgiveness. *Grateful* for her wit and intelligence and the other like-gifts she'd passed on to her children, and *forgiveness* for her weaknesses. The two important words I held dear — gratitude and forgiveness — along with what I'd learned long ago were the foundation, strength, and lifelines that bind and continue to build all relationships.

And so I would pray. And long after I pled her eternal rest, I prayed for strength to find the answers needed to make wise decisions.

Thirty-one
May we bury our mother?

2006

"Slow down!" Caity screamed, crossing herself quickly in prayer before reaching for the dash. "You just busted that light! We're burying Mom, not me!" She settled back in the passenger seat, double checked her seatbelt, and cut her eyes at me.

I let up on the accelerator, glanced back over my shoulder and looked at the brown paper bag on the car seat. It held the urn of my mother's ashes. I smiled big at my sister. "Mom never complained about my driving."

"Yeah? Well that's because she was already riding her own mental roller coaster. And I don't like roller coasters, so slow down and stop driving like we're on one!" Caity stared out the window. "Where do you want to bury her?" she asked.

The morning had started out with casual sister conversation that found us reflecting on the lawsuit. It then took a sharp turn when Caity and I decided it was time to bury our mother's remains. The chat ended with us grabbing the urn off her bookcase and heading out the door. For over two hours, we'd been driving the back roads of Kentucky and the streets of the city, trying to decide where to bury her.

I pulled the car over and let my tires kiss the curb before pulling hard on the emergency brake. "You said the orphanage grounds, but that's impossible. It's all subdivision now."

"Someone said a part of a wing is still standing."

"Caity, it would be fitting to place her in the grounds of our childhood home, but I'd rather not get arrested for digging up some anal retentive, homeowner's flower garden. It's all suburbia."

Caity laughed. "Pull up to the first house and ask, 'May we bury our mother alongside your pool between your rhododendrons and azaleas?'"

"Hah! Now that's wicked. Hmm, what about the Sisters of Charity's Motherhouse?" I raised a brow and offered a grin.

Caity rolled her eyes. "She'd probably come back and haunt us. No. You know how much Mom hated us being Catholic. We were only baptized because of the orphanage." She frowned. "Well, that and the pressures put on her from her cousin, Cecilia, a Mercy nun."

"Bingo!" I grinned.

"Kimmi? What—?"

"We're going to Church." I eased the car off the curb and merged into traffic. "We're giving her to the Catholic Church."

Four Catholic churches and three counties later we walked back to my car. "They're all locked," I said, "and it's getting late. Sheesh, you'd think they'd all be open in case you needed to pray or something. A Saturday and no church is open." I glanced back over my shoulder at the church, then stopped and grabbed Caity's arm. I pointed. "Look over to the right of the church's entry doors. See the statues? I believe that's Saint Gabriel and beside him is Saint Francis of Assisi."

Caity shifted the bag with the urn to her other arm and followed my finger. She smiled then turned to look at me.

"Mom loved animals," we both chorused. "And," I held up a finger, "Remember that St. Gabe is one of God's great messenger angels. He can announce Mom's final resting place."

We hurried over to the large statue of Saint Francis surrounded by chipped concrete animals. I studied the small garden surrounding the tableau. The garden was clearly suffering the effects of the summer's drought.

"I'm thinking those flowers need some strong fertilizer." I took the bag from her, pulled out the ornate urn, and shoved the empty bag into her hands.

Caity glanced around nervously. "Water," she murmured, trying to suppress a grin.

"Hmph, water, fertilizer." I shrugged. "No matter. What is it? You said having the ashes in your house depressed you and really she should have been buried years ago."

Caity looked over to the red church doors. "She was Methodist." She fumbled with the paper bag. "Kimmi, can we get arrested?"

"Pftt. We're Catholic! It's a life sentence! And Catholic orphans, courtesy of Mom." I raised a brow, then smiled at a passing policeman in his cruiser. "Hmm, traffic's pretty heavy today," I teased. I welcomed this light mood that had invaded our mission instead of the usual dark that usually hung around when we revisited anything having to do with our past.

Caity squirmed, and I laughed and hugged her. "Now, I say we give of our time, talent, and treasure, like the good Catholic shepherds we are." I coughed gently and grinned. "This garden needs fertilizing." I rubbed my hand over the raised painting of the urn and turned it upside down. "How does it open, Cat?"

Caity pulled her keys out of her purse, took the urn from me and started chipping away at the bottom of it. "How would I know? It's not like I've sat and sifted through her ashes before." She grimaced. "I think this is the opening," she said, tapping a raised square piece of ceramic.

A half hour later, I had my keys out, trying my hand at prying it open. Exhausted, we finally gave up and plopped down on the grass beside Saint Francis. Caity stared at the church, then gave a disgusted grunt. I placed the urn beside me and stretched out on the grass. My eyes focused on the tall cross on top of the dome of the church. I turned to Caity, laughed, then rolled my head back and forth on the ground's bluegrass.

"And she would've made such a great Catholic." I sniffed loudly, then chuckled.

My sister couldn't hold back for long. We laughed until tears streamed.

"Do you realize how ludicrous this is?" I asked. "Really, sharing a sisterly lunch would have been enough. Mom's probably laughing right now. She'd appreciate this quandary with her wonderful sense of humor."

"More like warped and wicked." Caity chortled.

"And like this isn't?"

I wiped away a laughing tear. A couple passed by and lowered their heads when my eyes met theirs. This caused another hysterical round of laughter between Caity and me.

Sitting up, I reached for the urn and twisted its top. It turned easily. Caity grabbed it from me and jumped up.

"Oh, my," I whispered, "it was that easy."

Caity lifted the plastic bag from inside the urn. Ashes blew in the wind and landed on my arm. I gasped.

"Stop. Stop it, Caity!" I grabbed her arm as she began to pour the ashes. "Nooo!"

Caity clinched the bag of ashes and I let out of sigh of relief, then we both had another fit of laughter.

"Cat," I suppressed a giggle with my hand, shook my head to shake the laughter and squared my shoulders. I took a deep breath and looked at the church. "We need to make this more ceremonial." I nodded. "More Catholic. You know, kneel and pray," I whispered.

Caity gave me a look of impatience, then conceded. I took her arm, lowered her to a kneeling stance beside me, then nudged her and said, "Pray."

Caity looked over her shoulder at the busy traffic of passersby. "Let's hurry," she whispered.

We stumbled over the words of The Lord's Prayer, crossed ourselves and asked God to give our mother peace. Then we stood and Caity poured the remaining ashes over the flowers. I said an additional, powerful prayer for God to grant me strength and forgiveness for my mother, then crossed myself again.

I hugged Caity and placed the expensive urn to the side of the church's door, hoping it could be put to use. I could sense Caity's peace as we drove away from the church. I turned the car into a parking lot and stopped.

"You want to eat now?" Caity asked.

I reached for the door latch. "No, not really. But I'm thinking perhaps a dip of praline pecan would be very nice about now."

She grinned. "It was Mom's favorite."

"Chocolate for me, but today I have a sudden craving for praline pecan. We can have sort of a toast in her memory and a catharsis in the true physical sense. And a homily, so to speak." I winked. "We did forget the homily, ya know?"

Caity's eyes were smiling for the first time in a long time.

I answered back with a smile.

Later that night, in the quiet of my peaceful home, I thought about answers and unanswered questions that have remained throughout my life. How I'd often reflected on my final departure day from the orphanage, the final farewell hug from Sister Charlotte, and that last visit, with no more clarity than before.

By all rights, my life should have ceased long ago. I don't know how I cheated death. Perhaps the invisible hands of God's angels have guided the cautious steps I'd taken on perilous, forked paths. Maybe God chooses people for good things in life as well as bad.

Many times, I've felt that being born into an impoverished third-world country would certainly have given me equal odds.

Still, I was grateful—very much so. There had been bumps, some bigger than others. Many times I've tempted fate. I've foolishly mocked death with my daring, youthful escapades. I've sought and obtained a higher education, held both insecure and secure jobs, and respected the difference between work and play. I know how to be brave but am okay with being afraid sometimes too. I welcome mistakes and glean knowledge from them.

But one day, I talked to fate and gave my heart to a man whose passion would mold and blend with my own. A man who brought me to my knees, gave me honor, and made me humble. And I would take Joe's hand and journey through time's door in a constant state of wonder.

Sometimes, one is given only a few seconds in life to control fate, kiss chance, and the timing of the moment is crucial to harmonizing it with His second.

Thirty-two
William

2007

I touched the swelling crocus bud and smiled. Just a little over a year ago, I had sat in darkness while the groundhog saw his shadow, and I'd felt as if I had lost my own.

Peering out my window, I had seen winter's bleakness, the warted barks of brown naked trees and sleeping grasses. I'd heard cold winds whistle and snake between glass panes, and wrapped myself tighter in flannels, fleece, prayer, and hope. I'd wept a dove's mournful cry and waited for another spring song, another chance to fortify my writing voice.

Today, winter's grip had finally worn off, shed her icy cloak and whisked away my sorrows. The light of spring had eased my journey back to pen and paper.

Rich black soil bared its face to the sun and birthed tender green crocuses as I stood outside, breathing in the first promise of a new season. And although the air was still slightly cool, warmth emanated from rays of spring sunshine. Birdsong had increased and small wildlife scampered about, free as the laughter of small children bouncing off suburban houses. These simple things, free for us all to enjoy, are like balm to one's bruises.

I hugged these sights and sounds tightly to myself as bad news came to me. The Church had taken a fall, cracking its mighty shield of respectability and leaving it vulnerable. I was concerned.

In early 2007, a federal judge issued an historic decision to William McMurry by refusing to dismiss a nationwide class action lawsuit against the Vatican alleging a cover-up to protect priests who molested American children. If the Court's decision is upheld on appeal, it will open the door for William to take depositions of Vatican officials, even the Pope. William based his claim on a secret 1962 Vatican directive, a "smoking gun," as he called it, ordering all bishops to keep secret any knowledge of priests' sexual abuse of children. Father Thomas Doyle, a strong clergy abuse advocate for survivors and canon lawyer would say, ". . . it is evidence of the Catholic's Church's obsession with secrecy."

Joe came and stood beside me, admiring the signs of early spring. I marveled at his honor, devotion and love for me.

"How's the book coming?"

"There are good days, and, well, there are the others, but the good days outweigh." I grinned and gave him a kiss.

"Ah," he said with a smile, "happy to see today's a good day. By the way, did you catch that article last month in the paper? McMurry's?"

"Yes." I rested my head comfortably on his chest. "I hope he makes it to the Vatican, Joe." He nodded and then wrapped me tightly in his arms.

I'd gained a newfound sense of freedom. William's voice had given me my own, and I wondered if he'd ever truly realize the magnitude of his gift. I was thankful to God that He'd given William to me and to the others. More importantly, through gaining and strengthening my lone voice, I felt my own faith restored and made whole again, even though I still have work to do on some of those forgiveness issues.

That day, I breathed a sigh of relief and silently toasted William. God-speed, William McMurry. Stay the course, and remain true to your path. As will I.

Thirty-three
As long as there is chocolate, there will be epilogues —
Life's good like that.

2010

The stench of brimstone assaulted me, and I could swear I tasted the sulfur of long-gone well waters and the bland oats.

And. I. Knew. I had to be near Satan's favorite food.

Small tremors threatened to quake. My heart quickened as I choked back the panic. I became shaky, gripping the cart's handle as uncertainty stepped in, and I prepared for fight or flight. Determined, I gritted my teeth and pushed forward. I merged slowly into the next curve and made my way down the cereal aisle at my local supermarket.

This time I forced myself to stop in front of the various packages of oatmeal. Usually I hurried past, giving them not so much as a glance. It was a habit I'd developed long ago. The smell amplified and threatened to devour me. My stomach rebelled, somersaulted, and I swallowed hard. Then, my eyes came to rest on orderly shelves. I stared for the longest time, willing calm. Mentally I raised my fist to shake at fear, and soon defiance grounded me.

A curiosity awakened as I took a closer look at the shelves, and I found myself amazed at all the different varieties of oatmeal, as well as its varied and colorful packaging. The different flavors mesmerized. There was apple, cinnamon, berry, vanilla and even chocolate! I took a small step forward and hesitantly reached for a brown box of vanilla.

A hurried mother with a child startled me as they whizzed by. I quickly set the package of oatmeal on its shelf, took a step back and gazed at the vivid packages.

Did I really need more oatmeal tears? After all, I was no longer anyone's victim, I was a survivor, strong, and any further foolish validation from eating oatmeal would not make me stronger. I straightened my shoulders and breathed.

I scanned my memories of my old Home-Sweet-Home, the orphanage. And I thought. How could one place have held so much peace, yet been so violent? Been so quiet, yet so loud? Have so much beauty, but hold so much ugliness? How? Years of hidden secrets and chilling horrors. And for it all, I'd received a pauper's share for each day's memory.

Yes, I'd calculated the settlement sum out for amusement. About enough money to purchase a small truckload of oatmeal packages and have them delivered to the Sisters of Charity's Motherhouse. The nuns would've preferred the plain variety. I couldn't help but smile at the thought.

A shopper's cart lightly bumped me and brought me back. Murmuring an apology over my shoulder, I took a tiny step forward and again looked at the grocer's stocked shelves.

I studied an animated Quaker character on one of the oatmeal packages and frowned. Leaning in closer, I let out a gasp. *Strange.* Strange how the Quaker character's starched uniform and hat resembled the outfits of my former child care givers. Peering at the character's face, I carefully considered the Quaker's closed smile.

"Sweet cartwheeling Jesus, he's smirking," I whispered. "Indeed."

I glanced around, turned back to the shelf, and picked up the package of oatmeal. I held it like one might hold a snake. Slowly, I shook my head and gave my best smirk, then childishly, I stuck out my tongue at the advertising character and a small smile formed on my lips. I placed the offending package back in its place.

Walking briskly away, I headed toward the bakery section. I scanned the selection of fresh baked goods. Grinning widely now, I reached for the warm box of glazed chocolate doughnuts and headed home to my family — my *forever* family.

Afterword

William F. McMurry
Attorney At Law

Louisville, Kentucky

In 1922 the Vatican sealed the fate of thousands of American children when it issued a secret written order requiring every Roman Catholic Bishop to keep the sexual abuse of children by clergy a Pontifical Secret. This secret decree, known as The Pontifical Secret, also made it a crime for priests to commit sexual abuse of minors. Everyone with knowledge of child sexual abuse accusations, including bishops and archbishops, was forbidden from telling anyone outside of the Vatican's Congregation for the Doctrine of Faith. This Congregation, or administrative department of the Holy See, was charged with the responsibility of prosecuting such crimes within the Roman Catholic Church.

This order, known as Supremae S. Congregationis S. Officii, is the official legislative text issued by the Congregation of the Holy Office and was approved by Pope Pius XI. The document is a reflection and written manifestation of the longstanding policies and directives of the Holy See regarding clerical sexual abuse, which impose this extreme level of secrecy not only on those within the Church who were to prosecute such cases but also on the document itself.

In 1964 the Vatican issued Crimen Sollicitationis (its title refers to the crime of solicitation of penitents in the confessional). While virtually identical to Supremae, this order replaced the 1922 directive and required each bishop to take an oath of secrecy under penalty of eternal damnation and excommunication. However, by the year 1964 virtually every one of the United States had criminal laws in place making it a crime to fail to report to law enforcement authorities known or suspected child sexual abuse. Notwithstanding the criminal laws of their state, the bishops feared eternal damnation more than they feared the unlikely prosecution for their failure to report abuse. These Vatican directives explain the choreographed movement of abusive priests from one parish to the next in an effort to avoid scandal and to fulfill their oath of secrecy.

When Kim was placed in the Sisters of Charity of Nazareth Orphanage in bucolic Anchorage, Kentucky (1960) there was no chance her abuse or the serial sexual and physical abuse of hundreds of other children would ever be discovered outside the institution. Kim's story is a grim but consistent account of the young lives of countless Catholic children unfortunate enough to be abandoned by society. With nowhere to turn for comfort, few children would survive their childhoods without major depression, drug addiction, dementia, or imprisonment.

The damaging effects of unreported childhood sexual abuse extend far beyond the individuals involved. Sadly, as many of these children age, their familial and employment relationships fail, and their dysfunction creates an enormous ripple effect of pain and hardship. The Vatican's doctrine of secrecy and the systematic silencing of those who would have reported these crimes have created an economic burden on our society.

Kim's story is not that of just a survivor, but of a rare spirit that simply could not be broken. Her story is important; for never in American jurisprudence has a Roman Catholic order of Nuns paid a monetary settlement for decades of institutional sexual abuse. In all, forty-five children, now adults, received recognition for their brave suffering.

Kim's book will empower all of us to look beyond the cloak of secrecy of any institution responsible for the protection of children.

More information regarding Mr. McMurry, including the current status of his Vatican case can be viewed at his website - www.courtroomlaw.com

Letter of Apology Request

Spring 2010

I've just hung up the phone. It's late and the conversation with yet another clergy abuse survivor has zapped my strength and spirit as they've recounted to me the horrors of their youth. I look to the clock and know I should be heading to bed because tomorrow is Easter. Easter. The celebratory feast day that millions of Catholics will spend rejoicing and celebrating the resurrection of Jesus.

I know also that the survivor I just spoke to will *not* be attending Church tomorrow, instead the victim of clergy abuse will struggle to get out of bed and spend most of the day weeping . . .

Just as I know; *Jesus* weeps.

~~~

4.11.2010 publication
by Kim Michele Richardson
Special to the Courier-Journal

I was deeply troubled when I read that Pope Benedict XVI was "weary and sad." I, too, am weary and sad. Let me explain. I've been answering calls, letters, and e-mails from countless victims of child abuse by the clergy for over a year now — calls, letters, and e-mails that the pope and the Catholic Church's hierarchy should be answering. So I thought I would send a polite reminder: Apologies and accountability are due.

I am a survivor of clergy abuse. Abandoned to a Catholic orphanage as an infant, for nearly a decade I was exposed to unspeakable abuses by Catholic nuns and a Catholic priest. It was only in the last year that these horrific abuses were publicly exposed that I was finally able to write about the long nightmare inflicted by those who hid behind His cloak to mask their evil deeds — deeds the Roman Catholic Church concealed while enabling decades of child abuse by predator clergy.

I wanted to forgive them and I did; however, I am often asked: How can you offer forgiveness to those who hide behind their righteousness, behind ill-conceived surety of their place in heaven and on Earth, those who have not asked for forgiveness because they do not think they need forgiveness?

Along with tens of thousands of victims globally, I am still waiting. We are waiting for an apology and an admission of accountability from the pope and the Church's hierarchy.

We've waited, sometimes for decades. People like the CEO, also a former orphan and victim of clergy abuse, who has to lock himself in his office because he's having a "bad day."

His "bad days" happen when the memories of physical and sexual abuse become too strong for him to function as a regular working adult. He writes to me hoping I can offer him strength, hoping I can make sense of crimes committed against him as a child that were the most heinous crimes committed in history.

Then there is the former priest who writes to tell me of rape by his "own." There's a nun, too. There is also the woman who suffers from crippling PSTD because of her abuses by clergy. She writes that she may not be contacting me for a while because she will probably be back in a "dark place" and will have to seek mental health institutional care for her "latest bout" — a bout directly caused by predator clergy. She prays she'll be strong and not be tempted again to commit suicide, as she's tried so many times before.

And before I forget, there's the strong advocate for victims of clergy abuse I've been privileged to know. He was not abused, but sadly, he is now "religiously empty," this man from a strongly connected religious background. I worry about him and his children.

There's also the daughter (one of five). Her mother, now deceased, a childhood resident of a Catholic orphanage, was severely abused and raped by clergy. The daughter says her mother's former clergy abuse touched everyone in her family and continues to cause trauma and discord so intense they have all sought counseling.

Pope Benedict XVI and the church's hierarchy have created a scatter bomb. Abuse. The abuse of one does not just stop with one, it also affects and harms their families, friends, co-workers, and society and on and on—so serious that it must be diffused. To do this, the church must be willing to publicly help these deeply wounded, still-suffering victims and survivors. Start the cleansing by reaching out to us, answering and also disclosing the records of predator clergy that have been protected by the Roman Catholic Church for decades.

My name is Kim Michele Richardson. I am waiting, along with all those voices around me.

The Apology

Sent: Tuesday, June 08, 2010 10:27 AM
Subject: Kim Michele Richardson

Dear Ms. Richardson,

On behalf of the U.S. Embassy to the Holy See, our Embassy has forwarded your (newspaper) letter, (2010.11.4.) on this subject to the Vatican.

The matter of sexual abuse of minors is of the utmost importance to the U.S. Government. The sexual abuse of anyone, anywhere, is abhorrent. It is especially troubling when allegations of abuse are directed at people who work in a position of trust with young people. On May 11, 2010, Pope Benedict XVI stated that "The greatest persecution of the Church does not come from the enemies outside but is born from the sin in the church." He added, "The church has a profound need to relearn penance, to accept purification, to learn on the one hand forgiveness, but also the necessity of justice. And forgiveness does not substitute justice."

We appreciate your time and express sympathy for your pain.

J. Nathan Bland
Public Affairs Officer
U.S. Embassy to the Holy See
Tel. (39) (06) 4674-3441
Fax (39) (06) 575-8346

ACKNOWLEDGEMENTS

Thank you to wonderful writing friends George Berger, Alice Loweecey, Jamie Mason for exceptional cheer-leading skills and encouragement.

My deep appreciation to Father Tom Doyle for your boundless energies, commitment and generous support to the countless survivors of clergy abuse.

I am forever grateful to my kind and supportive agent, Stephany Evans.

To my two beautiful children, my most precious gifts, I love you more.

To my husband, my always, I love you like salt loves meat.

To you, Treasured Reader: I thank you most.

The Unbreakable Child Readers Guide

1. Brutal child abuse stalks Kim Michele Richardson's, *The Unbreakable Child* like a flesh and blood monster. Try to imagine the constant beatings Kim endured from the nuns and priest for nearly a decade. What would a life of completely unexpected and dangerous blows, kicks, and slaps and molestations be like? After the newspaper photograph debacle, why did the nuns hide Kim away? How do you explain the various disappearances of the orphans, including Kim's sister, sometimes for lengthy periods? What kind of diet were the orphans routinely fed? Remember, for example, Kim's bewilderment with her first ice cream cone. Discuss, also, the terrifying use of drugs on the orphans.

2. Think about the art incident, when Sr. Daniel displayed Kim's "abstract" painting for two weeks, to Kim's utter mortification. What about Sr. Charlie locking her door to the young Kim experiencing witch nightmares?

3. Reflect on the spiritual abuse of the orphans. Think, for example, of the long-term effects of being told repeatedly, "Bad girls go to hell." What was Kim's typical experience at the obligatory Masses? Did the Catholic clergy do anything to foster the religious faith of the orphans? Did the nuns encourage racial justice at the orphanage?

4. What were the causes of profound silence exhibited by the orphans? Discuss Kim's continued habit of sitting on her hands to this day and sleeping on her abdomen?

5. When you reflect upon the issue of faith in Kim's life, are there clues in The Unbreakable Child as to the level of her belief? Thinking about her "birthday cake' prayers and also prayers buried in the playground; who wears the face of God in Kim's story?

6. As six-year-old Kim said she was "....nurturing the strength of my spirit with small rebellions. I could outlast them because time was on my side. They knew it and I knew it. And I knew that I'd never be completely broken." Did the certainty of survival that she had as a young child contribute to Kim's ability to rise above the abuse?

7. After Kim's First Holy Communion, she spent an afternoon with Diane and referred to her as "the mother" instead of "my mother" suggesting that she didn't understand her relationship to Diane. Why do you think she referred to Diane this way? Why did she tell Diane that she and her sisters liked school? Did she think that Diane would not help her if she knew the truth?

8. When Kim was nine, after she had been sent away from Saint Thomas for a number of visits with prospective adoptive parents, she "started rebelling against the family visits away from Saint Thomas". She was "terrified to leave the orphanage's familiarity, no matter how ruthless, to be thrust into the unknown". What was the underlying cause of Kim's behavior? How was her reaction similar or different from that of other abused children or abused women you have heard of?

9. *The Unbreakable Child* at times reads like a twisted fairy tale. Kim and the other orphans lead Cinderella's life of ashes as the forgotten step-children of the Church, but there is no

Prince Charming in their childhoods. There is a fairy godmother, Mrs. Lindauer, but she has no magic wand. At other times, the orphanage appears to be a nineteenth century workhouse lifted straight from a Dickens' novel, Oliver Twist's gruel included. Think, also, of the wringer washing machines inexplicably still in existence there in the 1960s. How is it that the spiritual reforms of Vatican Council II seem not to have touched the orphanage at all? How is it that the orphanage appears to have existed out of time?

10. Kim's reference to her "always-silent, never-sharing voice" suggests that she kept the details of her early abuse hidden and was reluctant to share details with others, and she confirms that in various places throughout the book. Given her desire to keep her early childhood a secret, how was Kim able to get past her "never-sharing voice" to go through with the lawsuit and write her story?

11. Did burying the mother's ashes bring further healing to the girls?

12. William F. McMurry had "given voice to many victims before." Those victims had family to support them but in this case the forty-five victims were orphans. Comment on how the experience of the lawsuit for those with families to support them might differ from those who didn't.

13. In speaking in his Afterword about the children who had been placed in the Sisters of Charity Orphanage, William said that "With nowhere to turn for comfort, few children would survive their childhoods without major depression, drug addiction, dementia or imprisonment." Kim Michele Richardson is a wife, mother, and an active volunteer in her community. How was Kim able to rise above her horrific

experiences as a child? Is it nature or nurture that is the biggest contributor to our character?

14. Traditional knights in armor are present in Kim's book. Both her attorney, William, and her husband Joe, do appear not so much as rescuers in the classic sense but as solid participants in Kim's quest. Discuss their roles as gallant knights.

15. Discuss the power of love as salvation. "I love you like salt loves meat" has great significance to Kim and her husband. Explain its meaning. Discuss the symbolism of the two objects they gave each other regarding this motto.

16. Has reading The Unbreakable Child changed the way you think about forgiveness? Is there anything that cannot or should not be forgiven? What does it take for someone to be able to forgive what seems to be the unforgiveable?

Developed exclusively for *The Unbreakable Child* by:
Linda Hoye, Editor & Distribution Editor of Story Circle Book Reviews.org, **Website:** www.armsofadoption.wordpress.com
and
Mary Ann Ledbetter, Teacher and writer